W0036026

SAGE was founded in 1965 by Sara Miller McCune to support the dissemination of usable knowledge by publishing innovative and high-quality research and teaching content. Today, we publish over 900 journals, including those of more than 400 learned societies, more than 800 new books per year, and a growing range of library products including archives, data, case studies, reports, and video. SAGE remains majority-owned by our founder, and after Sara's lifetime will become owned by a charitable trust that secures our continued independence.

Los Angeles | London | New Delhi | Singapore | Washington DC | Melbourne

Advance Praise

'In this wonderful book, R. Anand provides practical advice that can help you make the most out of your life. Anand combines ancient wisdom and modern science, storytelling and compelling data, all in the service of helping you find more happiness as well as success.'

Tal Ben Shahar, *Author of Happier, who taught the most popular course on happiness at Harvard University, serial entrepreneur, international speaker*

'Happiness is a state of well-being—physically, mentally, socially, psychologically and emotionally. The book handles the topics extremely comprehensively with 10 chapters. This book addresses virtually every possible aspect—separate and distinct. Each chapter is well outlined. I strongly recommend this book to everyone who wants to be happy—emotionally and psychologically.'

H. K. Chopra, *Chief Cardiologist, distinguished author and editor of cardiology journals and Past President, Cardiology Society of India*

'Anand has explored the theme of happiness in a fascinating manner, building upon psychological concepts and presenting real-world dimensions. This is an ideal playbook for all urban professionals as they embark on critical decision-making junctures several times in their career trajectories and go through a vortex of emotions. This is where Anand's book delivers a solid impact and makes an exhilarating read. This book in my opinion is a must-pick as a "transition coach" for all professionals dealing with high-stakes personal decisions in their careers.'

Tarunesh Madan, *Partner, Amrop—Executive Search, Board Practice and External Successors (Amrop is the world's largest retained executive search firm)*

'If happiness is something that you have been seeking or are interested to know more about, look no further. Anand, an industry veteran, brings you a book that decodes happiness at work along with our conscious and unconscious behaviours and actions. Real-life examples of work and home situations along with tools to understand, apply and practise enable reader to self-analyse an important and complex concept with simple and in-depth tools and undertake the journey to well-being. This is an important and must-read book for both individuals and practitioners who are interested in the concept of happiness.'

Amit Malik, *Chief People, Operations and Customer Services Officer, Aviva India*

'As a musician and simultaneously a corporate executive, both worlds' come together when I hear the RJ on a popular channel sympathizing on a Monday morning with the weary white-collar worker. The powerful concepts in this book should ideally be used by readers to obtain insights into their current state. They can then take the steps towards happiness and fulfilment that most of us yearn for but almost never discover. I firmly believe that holistic happiness and an ability to experience our world in its entirety are precious gifts we can discover as Anand takes us on this journey.'

Krishnan Chatterjee, *Musician, and Head of Marketing, Indian Subcontinent, SAP*

'It is rarely that we come across a book which creates a symphony of science and the art of living! The book is contemporary and much needed in today's complex as well as exciting era. Readers will find a unique work that helps them find inner peace, a centred personality and also a guide to take personal and professional decisions. The author has worked hard to explore multiple areas of scientific research for baselining, exploring and enhancing individual happiness and well-being. The many threads of being well that this book weaves is certain to attract future work in this area.'

Dhananjay Singh, *Director General,*
National Human Resources Development Network (NHRDN)

HAPPINESS at WORK

HAPPINESS at WORK

Mindfulness, Analysis and Well-being

R. ANAND

Los Angeles | London | New Delhi
Singapore | Washington DC | Melbourne

First published in 2018 by

SAGE Publications India Pvt Ltd
B1/I-1 Mohan Cooperative Industrial Area
Mathura Road, New Delhi 110 044, India
www.sagepub.in

SAGE Publications Inc
2455 Teller Road
Thousand Oaks, California 91320, USA

SAGE Publications Ltd
1 Oliver's Yard, 55 City Road
London EC1Y 1SP, United Kingdom

SAGE Publications Asia-Pacific Pte Ltd
3 Church Street
#10-04 Samsung Hub
Singapore 049483

Published by Vivek Mehra for SAGE Publications India Pvt Ltd, typeset in 10/14 pt ITC Stone Serif by Fidus Design Pvt. Ltd., Chandigarh and printed at Chaman Enterprises, New Delhi.

Library of Congress Cataloging-in-Publication Data
Name: Anand, Rajaganesan.
Title: Happiness at work: mindfulness, analysis and well-being / R. Anand.
Description: First Edition. | Thousand Oaks: SAGE Publications India Pvt Ltd,
    [2018] | Includes bibliographical references.
Identifiers: LCCN 2018029094 (print) | LCCN 2018031047 (ebook) |
    ISBN 9789352808076 (Web PDF) | ISBN 9789352808069 (E Pub 2.0) |
    ISBN 9789352808052 (pbk.: alk. paper)
Subjects: LCSH: Job satisfaction. | Stress management. | Mind and body. | Meditations.
Classification: LCC HF5549.5.J63 (ebook) | LCC HF5549.5.J63 A523 2018 (print)
    | DDC 650.1—dc23
LC record available at https://lccn.loc.gov/2018029094

ISBN: 978-93-528-0805-2 (PB)

SAGE Team: Manisha Mathews, Sandhya Gola, Megha Dabral and Anupama Krishnan

This book is dedicated to my children, Ananya and Kaushik. I wish they lead a happier life by accessing and applying the exploding knowledge on happiness. This book is also dedicated to readers who are seeking proven ways to happiness and wishing to gift this know-how to their next generation.

Thank you for choosing a SAGE product!
If you have any comment, observation or feedback,
I would like to personally hear from you.

Please write to me at **contactceo@sagepub.in**

Vivek Mehra, Managing Director and CEO, SAGE India.

Bulk Sales

SAGE India offers special discounts
for purchase of books in bulk.
We also make available special imprints
and excerpts from our books on demand.

For orders and enquiries, write to us at

Marketing Department
SAGE Publications India Pvt Ltd
B1/I-1, Mohan Cooperative Industrial Area
Mathura Road, Post Bag 7
New Delhi 110044, India

E-mail us at **marketing@sagepub.in**

Get to know more about SAGE
Be invited to SAGE events, get on our mailing list.
Write today to **marketing@sagepub.in**

This book is also available as an e-book.

Contents

Detailed Contents

Foreword

I feel very happy to be writing the foreword for *Happiness at Work: Mindfulness, Analysis and Well-being* authored by R. Anand, a practising HR leader with about two decades of experience. I have known Anand for many years now, and we have done a few projects together for larger causes. I do know about his keen interest and work in the areas of psychology, behavioural economics as well as his innovative approaches to people development. I was pleasantly surprised when I learnt that he has put down all the research and learnings to help individuals be happier—a worthy cause indeed!

In my own journey as an HR and business leader, spanning almost four decades, one key challenge has been how to motivate ourselves and our teams to perform as much as we can perform, to grow as much as we can grow, to be engaged and happy as much as we can be. I have often asked myself if there is a better way to do things that leaves individuals happy, contented and with a sense of accomplishment while making their organizations effective and competitive.

In my leadership journey, if there is a single learning which got strengthened over the years, it is the need for leaders to be conscious of the emotional and psychological states of themselves and their teams. Unfortunately, leaders are over-obsessed with only the business quotient of their leadership profile. If leaders are flexible and aware of their own and others' emotional and psychological states, they will make far bigger impact on happiness as well as success. This is where I think this book authored by Anand is going to bring the much needed focus to the emotional and psychological quotient of one's lifestyle. Anand has done well to first profile the reader to bring up this awareness. The book helps us to better listen, acknowledge, appreciate, recognize, nurture, empower and lead—ourselves and others.

When younger professionals ask how they can be happier and more successful, though they ask this question in many different ways, we in turn ask ourselves the following questions. How do I help them see the world with clarity, without distortions or delusions? How do I help them engage in a psychologically healthy manner with their challenges and opportunities? All of us, I and my peers across the industry must have coached and counselled by reflecting on how we dealt with the many questions and options that life has posed to us. However, there must be a more rigorous application of science, psychology and tested wisdom to these questions.

This book is just this rigorous application of science, psychology and wisdom. It profiles the external and internal theatres of the individual. It throws light on his/her often unconscious decision-making modes. It provides the theory and the tools and methods to attain optimum emotional, mental and psychological well-being. The work is extensive, comprehensive and practical. It utilizes situations that we face every day to discuss our potential pathways to well-being. Technically, the book's central approach is to remove distortions and adopt mindful practices to walk to one's own happiness. It is a thoroughly non-dogmatic and scientific approach.

The author has courageously revealed several aspects of his own life and predicaments to illustrate the practices he prescribes. I join him in expressing grateful thanks to the many individuals who have volunteered to tell their stories. Remember, these are normal professionals like you and me. This again makes the book interesting and applicable to urban professionals, to you and me.

Therefore, this book by Anand is an apt effort. It strives to facilitate much greater awareness, understanding and easy counter-measures to build in us better immunity against life's stressors and our flawed decision-making processes. An alumnus of IIT Madras, XLRI Jamshedpur and a serving board member of

NHRDN, Anand brings in a great passion to the subject and hence this book reflects his deep thoughts, knowledge, live corporate experience and research. The book from the first chapter 'Needle in a Haystack' to the tenth and the last chapter 'The Route and Milestones to Well-being' takes the reader, like a well-knit thread, on a smooth and silken drive filled with increasing curiosity and expectations.

I congratulate him for this rigorous and painstaking attempt and the publisher for bringing out this unique work on an important question for urban professionals.

S. Y. Siddiqui
Chief Mentor
Maruti Suzuki India Limited

Preface

This book is targeted at professionals in urban settings. Several of them wonder every day, as they commute to office, whether they could be happier. They question themselves: 'Can I pursue a greater joy?' 'Or, am I going to fade away?' Sometimes, they get a chance to escape into a vacation. They get an opportunity to not think about themselves and their daily chores. Sometimes, they think about the meaning of their lives during these vacations. When they are back, they deal with these vacuous questions again.

They deal with several stressors: family dynamics, parenting, 24/7 work, deadline pressure, health, financial stability, office politics, competition, long commutes, information overload, difficult bosses and strained personal relationships. When they do turn for help, they are overwhelmed with self-help literature. They often oversimplify these problems—'Do this and you can solve this problem.' There is a second category of self-help. They advocate that despite these stressors, you can practise some inner perfection and be happy.

Well-educated and sceptical professionals find these to be oversimplified and incomplete approaches as many of them are in denial and escapist in nature. Unless these professionals know why something works, their attempt to embrace the approach is half-hearted. If such exhortations come from a Guru they look up to, they might think 'maybe it works, but I don't get it'. In the end, these don't help attain happiness.

Advances in science, psychology, medicine, behavioural economics and re-application of philosophy to wicked problems do give us clear choices to make. And, everyone has a different starting point. One size does not fit all in our attempts at greater happiness. It is important to recognize that what happens in the outer theatre of individuals and how individual psyches are made both have a bearing on the happiness outcome. This is the foundational approach of this book. The interaction between the outer theatre and inner theatre produces stress or joy. The same prescription that works for one individual may not work for another.

Getting to well-being is hence a three-sided problem. There is a valid prescription which is only one-sided, applied to a defined set of situations that cause ill-being (opposite of well-being) and as you bring the two together, let us not ignore 'You'. Each of us is different. A prescription for happiness, similarly, will interact with us in unique ways. Unless we triangulate the individual, the situation and the well-being strategy, our success is a matter of chance. Indications and contra-indications, like in medicine, can tell you if you are progressing.

As a rational, sceptical person, I want to focus on the contradictory prescriptions of the experts and understand the boundary conditions in which a certain prescription does or does not apply. For example, there are universal distortions that can be minimized with certain practices. However, there are personal distortions that can be uncovered by certain proven tools. Transactional analysis (TA), inadvertencies analysis and dream analysis are excellent sources of insight on personal distortions. On the basis of this insight, your progress to mindfulness and happiness is much better secured. You can choose the right meditation or hobby and make it work for you.

Apart from study and reflection, I have utilized the access to people my profession allows to look at the lives of 'normal people' in their own pursuit of happiness. While the profession allows you a certain legitimacy to ask and provides a cultural expectation that people reveal their vulnerabilities, hopes and fears, I am grateful to those individuals who chose to analyse their context in my presence. I have wondered if there is a way to make each one of them happier.

I hope my readers will deploy these practices and approaches to be happier. I also hope that readers will utilize these practices and approaches to bring up the next generation, convinced on the validity of these approaches.

Disclaimer: This work is a result of my study, observation, practice and reflection. The views, opinions and suggestions expressed in this book are mine and not of my employers and organizations—past and present.

Acknowledgements

I want to begin by acknowledging Santhosh, my walk buddy, for sowing the seeds of the origin of this project. We used to chat for hours in the course of our walks as to how the urban professional's life has become complicated. He would bring some studies and recommendations and I would point out the lack of rigour in those studies. We got talking about organizing the challenges for happiness faced by urban professionals. It is then that he referred to how I must have seen several of them in my profession. He suggested if I could tell them something from my knowledge of psychology and wellness, something that is proven. This was the origin of this work. I am grateful to him for not only sparking this thought but also for brainstorming the list of challenges.

I would like to acknowledge my father, Professor D. Rajaganesan, for helping me with the chapter on meditation and also for his critique of chapters that were based on psychoanalysis. He holds a PhD in psychoanalysis, having investigated the complexes around fatherhood! I would also like to thank my mother for not imposing her dreams onto her children.

I am grateful to Manisha Mathews of SAGE. The promptness with which she reviewed the work and commented subtly forced me to be prompt as well. She was able to logically push me to clarify more, investigate more as well as simplify. She also has a gift of holding you to a timeline without being seen as pushy. But for her, I would not have believed that this can be written amidst tight work schedules at the speed at which I have written this book.

I thank my teams and all 165 of them for taking pride in their work and pushing me logically so that nothing got stuck. I thank teams that supported me from the corporate office for their crisp resolution of issues, my bosses for understanding that I was pursuing a project of my passion. They never denied any leave that I applied. I often applied for leave at short notice whenever I got an internal momentum on this project. The many air travels I undertook also served to organize my thoughts and read or re-read the work's references.

I am ever thankful to the thousands of people who share their life with me, not only because I am their HR, but because of the trust and faith they repose in me as an individual. I am particularly thankful to those who offered me the permission to use a slice of their life to illustrate many points in this book. Since I have masked them, it will not be appropriate to name them. It is a unique situation where I wish to acknowledge them loudly but doing so will compromise their privacy. I hope they will read this paragraph and understand that I mean every word.

Last, no acknowledgement will be complete without thanking my spouse, S. K. Kripa. She is a pillar of strength and dependability. She does not fancy her spouse to be an intellectually absorbed person but wishes him to participate in life with her on small and big matters. She also knows how to give space and allow you to be yourself. She carried the load of running the house and I wish to unburden her a bit more from now on.

1

Needle in a Haystack

What is good Phaedrus and what is not good, need we ask anyone to tell us these things.

There are as many prescriptions about the 'way to well-being' as there are pundits. No surprises. The subject of well-being, our own well-being, is so immediate and so important that we are eager to try whatever works.

The range of what we mean by 'well-being' is very wide. What is well-being for one who has just attempted suicide? What is well-being for a student about to appear for his board examinations? What is it for a working woman balancing multiple priorities? Is it the same for a rich and healthy adult trying to pursue his/her hobby? A single definition cannot do justice to a vast variety of situations.

What is common is that the journey of well-being is a journey to get emotionally and mentally fitter. The spectrum of situations is so vast that even the psychologists have divided their world into two sub-disciplines. There is a clinical psychology that focuses on curing the sick and there is a positive psychology that helps normal people get even better. The positive psychologists are now intent on proving that what gets the sick cured cannot get the happy to be happier.

Defining Well-being

Defining well-being or happiness seems to be a more complicated project compared to attaining it! For a moment, we will use 'well-being' and 'happiness' interchangeably. The warmth of the sun on your skin on a cold winter morning makes you happy. So does the attention you enjoy on your birthday. Yes, you experienced happiness when you had been absorbed in your favourite game and noticed that many hours had passed when you 'came out'. Feeling energized after a brisk walk that stretched you to the right extent, the after-glow of good sex, counting your blessings as you finished a successful project or paying obeisance to God—which one of these happy states are we having in mind here?

The goal of well-being has also been cast as the absence of negative states—not being overwhelmed at work, a non-monotonous life, no fear of the future, no regrets about the past, not being ignored or bullied or harassed in the present moment and no sense of despair. By the way, philosopher Kierkegaard aptly defines the opposite of despair as 'the will to be one's true self' connoting a complete self-acceptance.

We have sought to understand the meaning of well-being by a quick survey of samples of experiences that would be accepted as its yard stick. Some prominent schools of thought have sought to define and pursue well-being.

The Stoics

Stoicism was a flourishing pre-Christian philosophy practised in Rome and Greece. 'The good life' was the stated pursuit of the stoics. They had the zeal to enjoy the pleasures as well as the subtler happiness that life offered but were equally pre-pared to face its worst adversities. They valued rationality over comforting but un-verified beliefs. They did not even assume a just world or a God who is trying to bring order in it. The Roman emperor Marcus Aurelius used stoicism to keep his head on his shoulders and tackle his immense responsibilities. 'Virtue' is the path to happiness, according to the stoics. Virtue is how we engage with the world and hence is totally up to us. The world will not work as per our desire and will. We must, however, assert our will and freedom by changing the things we can and accepting the things we cannot. The metaphor is that of a dog tied to a cart with a long chain. The dog can resist till the length of the chain but will soon be dragged by the cart. The dog can instead realize this and run along with the cart, enjoying the scenery along the way because it has wholly and rationally anticipated the world.

In the clear words of the stoic Epictetus, this rationality and fortitude will help man 'be sick and yet happy, in peril and yet happy, dying and yet happy, in exile and yet happy, in disgrace and yet happy'.

'Men are not disturbed by things, but by the views they take of them', sums it all up very nicely.

The Psychoanalysts

Sigmund Freud, one of the controversial yet towering figures of the 20th century, founded psychoanalysis. He subjected the human condition to the most rigorous and open-minded scrutiny, courageously pursuing bitter truths about ourselves than remaining content with comfortable half-truths. He influenced our understanding of the human psyche in immeasurable ways.

Freud discovered and adduced evidence for an unconscious region in our psyche. This region lies beneath the subconscious region. The conscious region is always open to us, for example, our name is in the conscious region. The subconscious is not so open; but we can, with some effort, access material in the subconscious region. An example would be what we had for dinner last night. The unconscious region is not accessible for such simple and direct attempts.

Freud also provided several tools to loosen the vice-like grip of our unconscious selves. According to him, we distort ourselves to the point that we no longer know what we are thinking and feeling. It is possible to analyse ourselves and these distortions, find their source and minimize their remote control on our behaviour and decision-making.

Freud was accused of being excessively preoccupied with the negative, unhealthy aspects of our psyche. Perhaps, only once he was posed this question of what is it like to be healthy. His response was insightful: The ability to 'love, work and play' is being psychologically healthy, Freud observed. He also traced our religious beliefs and several of our customs to unconscious impulses. According to him, civilization itself has extracted a price on our individual zest and happiness while giving order and security.

What makes psychoanalysis relevant for our present endeavour are the myriad tools that it has given us to access our unconscious psyche. The dreams that we dream and the inadvertencies that we commit give us glimpses into our vast, dark unconscious psyche.

The Philosopher: Bertrand Russell

Bertrand Russell was one of the tallest philosophers who lived in the previous century. He was a prolific writer on several themes relating to the human condition. His book *The Conquest of Happiness* was so popular that it gave him financial security for the rest of his life.

In this book, Russell defines 'happiness' at once in terms of both absence and presence of certain states of mind—an absence of emptiness or lack of meaning, too much boredom or excitement, the stress of competition, the burden of fatigue, envy, guilt, victim mindset and shame; and a presence of zest for living, affection, a family to go to, interesting work, wide interests in objects (not persons) and efforts towards a larger purpose. Russell perhaps wrote the first significant book on happiness in the modern western world and to this day is unparalleled for its systematic approach, common sense and clarity.

In his famous and stand-out prescription, he asks us to eschew a preoccupation with one's self. Contemplative practices like meditation are at the risk of promoting a preoccupation with one's own self. Instead, he asks us to embrace a zestful engagement with what the world has to offer, using one's skill and constructing something worthwhile. The route to well-being requires us to travel a certain path. Each one must work it out, and not think of 'Happiness as a sweet ripe fruit that will fall into our mouths', says Russell. It is an active pursuit. He became happier after he became indifferent to himself.

> And interest in oneself leads to no activity of a progressive kind. It may lead to the keeping of a diary, getting psycho-analysed, or perhaps becoming a monk. But the monk will not be happy until the routine of the monastery has made him forget his own soul.

This is Russell's view.

The Physician's Perspective

Since stress is treated by physicians directly or indirectly, this set of professionals have also attempted to offer their 'paths to well-being'. Like the psychoanalysts, the physicians too first focused on a pathology-therapy paradigm in their discussion on stress per se. Today, many of them are coming round to the non-pathological idea of well-being, even if there is no disease to cure per se.

Dr Amit Sood from the Mayo clinic is one such professional. He is amongst the experts who are trying to 're-wire our brains and minds' to be more happy. Negative feelings are an evolutionary hangover. They helped us be vigilant in the earlier phases of our phylogenetic history, writes Dr Amit Sood. Unfortunately, they are now dysfunctional in our much more secure contemporary environment. Our hardware, still from the past, defaults us to remembering negative things and treat positive experiences as fleeting. This tendency can be rewired or corrected by feeling secure, by feeling grateful every day in the morning for 21 days, says Sood. The gratitude exercise sets the default tone of our mental and emotional life and thus helps us tackle the world with lesser palpitations.

Dr Sood also talks about snapping out of stress at a given moment. He advocates two powerful exercises called 'joyful' attention and 'kind' attention. Joyful attention pretty much mirrors Russell's positive prescriptions on happiness and nicely translates this into an exercise we can all do. The idea is to engage with the world in all its vividness and nuance by simply noticing what is there in front of us.

'Kind' attention can be mapped on to several of the negative states that cause unhappiness in us that Russell refers to. Here, you greet a person by sending a secret wish for his/her well-being. Next, you reason their negative behaviour as arising out of their ignorance and compulsion.

Dr Sood is basically a physician and hence is able to help us relate to the mind–body connection through the case histories of many of his patients.

The Positive Psychologists

Martin Seligman is the father of the positive psychology movement. He spent a good number of early years of his career in clinical practice of psychology. He found something missing and narrow in the exclusive focus on curing—the negative approach of psychology. The negative states taxonomy evolved to make a precise and consistent diagnosis so as to facilitate medical insurance claims for mental disease treatments. There is an extensive taxonomy for the negative states.

Instead of researching disease and depression, he wanted to research happiness and other positive emotions. Professor Seligman is now on a mission to create taxonomy for the positive emotions. His first attempts to found positive psychology led him to focusing on the stress arising due to a sense of helplessness and building on the work of Albert Bandura, another psychologist.

Bandura did some experiments on animals: An animal kept in a box is subjected to mild electric shocks. In order to escape the shocks the animal tries to jump onto alternate platforms, but experiences shock in those platforms too. After a few attempts, the animal gives up the attempts to escape. After an interval of time, the experimenter presented the animal with some viable alternatives which would not lead to any experience of shock. The animal by that time had given up for good hope of a solution and preferred to withstand the shock rather than make attempts to escape it.

I had once observed a pigeon that flew in at our air-conditioned office when a door that automatically closes was left open for a long time by visitors. Trapped in a very narrow enclosure, it struggled to find a way out, circling anti-clockwise and displaying an agitated desperation. I opened a large French window, which must have been quite visible to the bird for it to escape. The window was on the very arc that the bird was flying. Having learnt to be helpless, it was simply circling around. This bird had learned to be helpless in a short period of time.

In human beings too, a similar pattern of reaction to repeated frustrations sets in. When we are confronted with negative events, we do two things.

We attribute a reason for these events and we also project this reasoning beyond those very events to our lives in general. This is a logical fallacy called 'Hasty Generalization'. We give typically these three reasons, one of it more frequently than others depending on our personality—'my incompetence', 'my enemies' or 'my fate'. Once we embrace such a belief, we become blind to the larger arc of the horizon of options spread around us. This is the first of our reactions, why did it happen?

Martin Seligman discovered that the way we interpret the events of our lives can have a major impact on our happiness. This is the second aspect of our reactions. How long and how pervasive is this negative state going to be? Some of us feel that a particular spell is going to last forever; others feel that it will be transient. Similarly, when something goes right or wrong in one aspect of our lives, the feeling that our entire life-world will either go right or wrong is also a typical attribution some of us make. He called this attitude, on whether something will or will not change with time, the 'temporality' dimension. The second notion that all aspects of our lives everywhere are at once coloured by the same tone, he called the 'globality' dimension.

The reason soothsayers and astrologers are able to work successfully on some of us is that they skilfully get us out of this learned helplessness. They acknowledge that we are going through a bad phase. Next, they specify a date when things will turn around for us. We accept such predictions, thanks to our desire to get out of it which also warrants our trust in them. Through this 'psychological trick', they win our trust and provide a hope for us. From this point, we start exploring alternatives instead of enduring our electric shocks.

Whether these are rational or irrational reactions is a topic of another debate, but certainly they increase or decrease our happiness. Professor Seligman coined the term 'learned optimism' or finding more reasons to be hopeful than hopeless in his first attempt to explore and articulate a positive psychology.

In his second thrust at positive psychology, Professor Seligman looked at the pursuit of 'authentic happiness' as the better goal to pursue. This broadened the concept of 'learned optimism'.

In his third thrust, he proposes 'well-being' as the more worthwhile goal. Well-being rests on the pillars of positive emotion, happiness, a zestful engagement with the world, trusted relationships, meaning and a sense of accomplishment. Well-being is flourishing, as against languishing. Happiness and positive emotions are necessary but not sufficient conditions for well-being. Within limits, one can be lower on a few components and compensate them on other components.

Martin's students, Shawn Achor and Tal Ben Shahar, have branched off and developed more prescriptions for the happy life. Sonja Lyubomirsky (*The How of Happiness and The Myths of*

Happiness) and Gretchen Rubin (*The Happiness Project*) have all articulated their version of their 'experiments with happiness'.

Mihaly Csikszentmihalyi, in his famous work *Flow: The Psychology of Optimal Experience*, aligns with Russell's concept of a preoccupation with the external. According to him, 'flow' occurs when one's skill gets stretched in the pursuit of a goal that is meaningful and in such absorbing task, one forgets oneself and this is the happy state. He studiously avoids making any value claim that everyone must pursue this 'flow'.

Mind–Body Connection

Lest the reader misunderstand well-being is all about emotional and psychological health, I wish to add the criticality of physical well-being and physiological health. A lot of our sense of self and even our thoughts, emotions and reactions originate in the body (the 'soma') giving the term psychosomatic illness to several stress-related ailments. If we are not hydrated (do not have enough water) or cannot regulate the level of sugar in the blood, we cannot hope to be at our creative best. In fact, studies have shown that low blood sugar level impels one to abandon problem-solving and often take snap/incorrect decisions. A famous study was performed by the researchers from Columbia University, New York City and the Ben Gurion University of the Negev at Israel by analysing 1,000 parole decisions. The study found the time of the day judges wrote their 'parole decisions' greatly influenced the decisions themselves: Just before the lunch hour, when the judges are hungry and their sugar levels are low, they are more likely to refuse parole compared to the judgements they wrote immediately after lunch or earlier in the day after breakfast. After a meal, our parasympathetic nervous system gets activated in an effort to digest our food. This is active when the cobra has just gobbled its rat. Some of you who have seen the cobra in the zoo after its meal in the afternoon can relate to this. Like the cobra's, our pulse rate slows down, and a calming, generous and relaxed mood state permeates our being after a meal. One is prone to consider the world in a favourable light right after food when one's stomach is full. Equally, when we are stressed, our foods take longer to digest, giving rise to regurgitation that is so often associated with acidity and wakefulness at night. The body and mind are not isolated systems but fairly interconnected ones. Within limits, one can leverage the somatic system with the psychic system and vice versa.

Body is not merely a lever for the mind but also a medium of expression for the mind: As a rule, the body communicates what the mind feels and thinks. The body has its own, non-verbal language of communication. So much so, body language has become a domain of study in its own right.

Desmond Morris has nicely explored this interconnectedness in his books *People Watching*, *The Naked Ape* and *The Human Zoo*. In *The Human Zoo* Morris draws a parallel between the competitiveness and posturing at office by human beings to the behaviour of animals in the forest as they compete for resources, food and mates. He advances a second principle pertinent to the mind–body connection. This is the principle of coherence. Un-expressed feelings that we repress, for example, we want to frown at our bosses but instead smile, are sure to resurface soon. We will be snapping at something else at the next opportunity. This is further explored in the operations of the unconscious by the psychoanalysts. The coherence principle also reinforces that we cannot fake our way into a good life; we need to anchor this strongly in reality.

Amy Cuddy has made popular the whole subject of body language and how it affects our sense of self and our thought processes and psychological orientation. It is now the basis of several executive coaching on 'presence'. Presence or 'executive presence' refers to the usage of non-verbal tools to interpersonal influence and for eliciting confidence in one's ideas and leadership.

The postures of our bodies and the pattern of our breaths are too critical to be happenstance. They influence our thinking, feeling and decision-making in addition to activating our organs for physical well-being.

It is no surprise that the yogic system of practices first starts with the asanas, which are manipulations of the body, before they go to *Pranayama* and onward to more meditative practices. They try to make us conscious of our kinaesthesis, how our body is placed relative to the world. They explore the partially conscious processes such as breathing and pulse after the asanas are perfected. Perhaps, a study of mental processes and making them conscious must have existed in the yogic system as well and lost in the passage of time.

Policy and Institutions

The pursuit of well-being is not only merely an individual affair. Individual well-being has far-reaching implications. It affects how we parent, how we teach, what institutions are good and what is the role of government and policy making. Thomas Jefferson, a Founding Father of the USA, author of the *Declaration of Independence* and the third president of the USA, said more than 200 years ago, 'The care of human life and happiness ... is the only legitimate objective of good government.' The need to discuss these implications has been globally recognized and is moving fast to the centre stage of every discourse. Did you know that *The United Nations Report on Happiness* is in its fourth edition? The report discusses policy and performance of several countries against a happiness index.

In this fourth edition of the report, the authors have scanned voluminous database pertaining to four countries—the USA, Britain, Australia and Indonesia—and have discerned six variables as 'the key determinants of happiness and misery'. The six variables are income, education, whether in a relationship with a partner, employment status, physical health and mental health. Across these countries, mental health was found to be a critical correlate of happiness. The ultimate question that measured happiness or misery was, 'Overall, how satisfied are you with your life these days?' This is a popular life satisfaction question measured on a 10-point scale. What is also interesting in this study is that it costs much lesser to solve the mental health problem of an individual compared to bringing about the necessary level of change in the other variables and make one more person happier.

There is an explosion of literature and surge in interest on well-being. This is now regarded as the umbrella concept. Happiness, engagement, positive emotions, feeling secure and having fellow mates who accept us unconditionally and have meaningful challenges to overcome with one's unique strengths are components of this conception. The references in this work can take the reader to such material. We will soon have plentiful prescriptions to choose from in the pursuit of our own well-being.

This, then, is the proverbial needle-in-the-haystack, now picked out by powerful computer programs rummaging over volumes of data under the guidance of experts engaged by no less than the United Nations Organization. How to navigate our individual pathways to pick the needle ourselves, each one of us severally, is the agenda of this book.

2

My Stress Profile

What are my stressors? How do I perceive them? What has my life predisposed me too? How much of the well-being inducing factors are present in my life? These are some of the questions we will introspect about in this chapter.

Please answer the following questions as honestly as you can. Your level of agreement to the statement can be expressed as '1' if you strongly disagree, '10' if you strongly agree and any of the numbers in between as per the descriptions provided. Use 'NA' if any of these items are not applicable to you. There is no right or wrong answer. An accurate profiling of your present life will help you deploy the most effective well-being strategy.

S. No.	Statement	1–Strongly disagree	2	3–Disagree	4	5–Neutral	6–Neutral	7	8–Agree	9	10–Strongly agree	NA–Not applicable
1	I have no one to help with the household chores											
2	I have no one to assist me in bringing up my children											
3	I have no one to turn to for my aged parents' well-being											
4	I/We struggle for acceptance in the community we live in											
5	I struggle for acceptance in my workplace											
6	It takes a lot of time to commute to and from my workplace											
7	I am unable to log out of work systems											

S. No.	Statement	1–Strongly disagree	2	3–Disagree	4	5–Neutral	6–Neutral	7	8–Agree	9	10–Strongly agree	NA–Not applicable
8	I plan for my workday when at home											
9	I rarely exercise											
10	I end up sitting for most of my workday											
11	My work has to be done sitting through all day											
12	I have to be on the alert for colleagues getting me into trouble at work											
13	I have to be on the alert for a boss who is trying to get me fixed											
14	My office meetings are full of put downs											
15	My office meetings are full of show-offs											
16	My project or work need to be justified with powerful sponsors who have a negative bias on the project											
17	I am often racing against time to meet work deadlines											
18	I am worried about health impact of pollution in my city											
19	I am worried about safety and security in public spaces											

S. No.	Statement	1–Strongly disagree	2	3–Disagree	4	5–Neutral	6–Neutral	7	8–Agree	9	10–Strongly agree	NA–Not applicable
20	I am worried about my children's safety and security at their school											
21	I am worried about my children's safety and security in public spaces											
22	I am lagging behind in news and current affairs											
23	I am behind critical information at office that impacts my success											
24	I have a load of information to assimilate for my work											
25	I cannot predict what it will take to sustain my current lifestyle											
26	I don't know the best way to invest my surplus											
27	I don't have anyone to turn to for parenting questions											
28	I argue with people who are important in my life											
29	I am unsure if my spouse reciprocates the same intensity of love											
30	I am unsure if my spouse reciprocates the same level of affection											
31	I feel I am not giving myself enough 'me-time'											

S. No.	Statement	1–Strongly disagree	2	3–Disagree	4	5–Neutral	6–Neutral	7	8–Agree	9	10–Strongly agree	NA–Not applicable
32	I feel uncertain about how my career will unfold											
33	I feel uncertain about how my personal life will unfold											
34	I feel uncertain about how my financial health will unfold											
35	I feel uncertain about how my physical health will unfold											
36	I feel I am not happy enough											
37	I feel I am depressed											
38	I feel a lack of energy											
39	I go through 'joyful' events absent-mindedly											
40	I am preoccupied when my children speak to me											
41	I feel I am not pursuing the career I should be											
42	I feel I am not pursuing the leisure activities that I should be pursuing											
43	I feel I am not pursuing the life I should be											
44	I feel bored											
45	I feel overwhelmed											
46	I feel I am wasting my time											
47	I fear that I will not live up to my own expectations											

S. No.	Statement	1–Strongly disagree	2	3–Disagree	4	5–Neutral	6–Neutral	7	8–Agree	9	10–Strongly agree	NA–Not applicable
48	I fear I will not live up to others' expectations											
49	I feel lonely											
50	I feel good times/luck are deserting me											
51	I feel a resentment towards colleagues in my work setting											
52	I feel a resentment towards my boss											
53	I feel a resentment towards my organization											
54	I feel guilty about not doing the right things											
55	I blame myself for botching up certain opportunities											
56	I have a strong urge to revisit certain decisions I have taken in the past											
57	I cannot express my true feelings at my workplace											
58	I cannot express my true feelings at home											
59	I cannot express my true feelings with friends											
60	I cannot access any friends to talk to											
61	I am worried for my children's career											
62	I am worried about my children's health											

S. No.	Statement	1–Strongly disagree	2	3–Disagree	4	5–Neutral	6–Neutral	7	8–Agree	9	10–Strongly agree	NA–Not applicable
63	My children have to be medicated continuously											
64	My spouse has to be medicated continuously											
65	I am living away from my spouse because of work											
66	I am living away from my spouse because of disagreements											
67	I skip breakfast											
68	I cannot access healthy foods											
69	I have to endure hunger											
70	I have to endure thirst											
71	I suffer from an embarrassing ailment											
72	I feel I am not settled in the right job											
73	I feel unsure I will ever be employed											
74	I feel envious about someone											
75	I feel the need to avenge a wrong											
76	I feel there is little meaning in life											
77	I often experience tiredness											
78	I fear I will be a loser											
79	I feel others are out to get me											

S. No.	Statement	1–Strongly disagree	2	3–Disagree	4	5–Neutral	6–Neutral	7	8–Agree	9	10–Strongly agree	NA–Not applicable
80	I fear I will be condemned by society											
81	I feel no one is affectionate towards me											
82	My work is monotonous											
83	I don't spend a decent amount of time on my hobbies every week											
84	I feel there is hardly anything interesting to come to know of											
85	I feel success is beyond my control											
86	I feel my future will be worse compared to my present											
87	I fear that my children have a bleak future											
88	I fear my spouse will have health issues											
89	I fear my spouse will be worse off compared to the present											
90	In workplace, I feel excluded in meetings											
91	In family and social settings, I feel excluded											
92	In family and social settings, I often get bullied or suppressed											

S. No.	Statement	1–Strongly disagree	2	3–Disagree	4	5–Neutral	6–Neutral	7	8–Agree	9	10–Strongly agree	NA–Not applicable
93	I feel unwanted attention on me causing a sense of insecurity											
94	I am stalked online											
95	I am stalked offline											
96	My children are stalked											
97	I feel anxious about what will happen tomorrow											
98	I feel a nervous excitement											
99	I feel guilty about certain acts I committed in the past											

100. On a scale of 1–10, how satisfied are you with your life these days, where '1' is most satisfied and '10' is least satisfied?

Outer Realm

After you have finished answering the questions, please compute your scores and put them in Table 2.1.

The first column titled 'LS' is your overall life satisfaction score. The lower it is, the better.

The next column titled 'S' is a summative assessment of your stress profile, and similarly low scores are indicative of a favourable assessment and high scores indicate an unfavourable self-assessment. An average score of 6 or higher means that

Table 2.1. Profiling My Outer Realm and Life Satisfaction

	LS	S	01	02	03	04	05	06	07	08	09	010	0
Statement Numbers	100	36, 37, 39, 40, 43, 50, 97	1, 2	27, 63, 64	28, 29, 30, 65, 66	25, 26	6	7, 8, 31	17	22, 23, 24, 45	18, 67, 68, 77, 9, 10, 11, 69, 70, 71	13, 16, 12, 15	01, 02, 03, 04, 05, 06, 07, 08, 09, 010
Average score (sum of scores/number of scores, ignore NA statements)													

you need to find out the causes and take decisions to move to well-being. A score of 5 or lower means that you are doing well. If you address the few minor irritants in your outer life and inappropriate reactions in your mental life, you can actually feel good.

Columns 01–010 represent factors in your outer life that may be causing you stress. They are elaborated in detail in the next chapter and captured in the following table.

Outer Theatre Factors	Factor Name
01	Family dynamics
02	Parenting
03	Relationship
04	Financial security
05	Commute
06	24/7 work
07	Deadline
08	Information overload
09	Health
010	Boss and office politics

Notice the average number for each of these factors. How many of them are greater than or equal to 7? Typically, if 3 or more of these 10 factors are greater than or equal to 7, the individual will experience high stress. Such individuals need to immediately intervene and ameliorate at least one of the factors.

Similarly, an average score of more than or equal to 6 calls for intervention.

Inner Realm

Please transcribe scores of the statements in Table 2.2.

Columns I1 to I9 represent factors internal to us. They might have originally arisen from our life conditions and other

Table 2.2. Profiling My Inner Realm and Life Satisfaction

	LS	S	I1	I2	I3	I4	I5	I6	I7	I8	I9	I
Statement Numbers	100	36, 37, 39, 40, 43, 50, 97	19, 34, 35, 79, 80	3, 20, 21, 61, 62, 87, 88, 89, 96	32, 33, 47, 48, 72, 73, 78, 85, 86	4, 5, 90, 91	14, 92	93, 94, 95	51, 52, 53, 75	55, 56	54, 99	I1, I2, I3, I4, I5, I6, I7, I8, I9
Average score (sum of scores/ number of scores, ignore NA statements)												

external variables. At this point, however, they are our default anxieties. These anxieties usually have a past focus—something about our pasts that we are unable to come to terms with. They may also have a future focus—about a catastrophe that may befall us or others we care about. Sometimes, these anxieties are present moment issues that produce disagreeable reactions. What makes these present moment issues internal is that they are viewed with the inner lens of exclusion or bullying or unwanted attention. The external circumstance may or may not warrant such a reaction.

The factors are elaborated in subsequent chapters, but the following table names these factors pertaining to the inner theatre.

Inner Theatre Factors	Factor Name
I1	Fear of self-harm
I2	Fear of harm to those we care for
I3	Fear of falling short
I4	Feeling excluded
I5	Feeling bullied
I6	Subjected to unwanted attention
I7	Feeling bitterness about the past
I8	Feeling regretful about the past
I9	Feeling guilty about the past

Unlike the outer theatre, even if one of the factors is self-assessed to be adverse (greater than or equal to 7), there is a case for undertaking some corrective action. Corrective action involves understanding the origin of these inner defaults. The very act of unearthing the source provides us with a conscious choice to reduce its sway over us.

Well-being Enablers

Please do transcribe the scores of the factors in Table 2.3 that support the occurrence of well-being. Do take care to follow the exact instructions.

Table 2.3. My Well-being Enablers and Life Satisfaction

	LS	S	WB1	WB2	WB3	WB4	WB5	WB6	WB
Statement Numbers	99	36, 37, 39, 40, 43, 50, 97	44, 98	74	42, 83	41, 46, 76, 82	49, 57, 58, 59, 60, 81	38, 84	WB1, WB2, WB3, WB4, WB5
Scoring	Value	Average excluding the NA items	Average of 2 (abs difference between score and 5)	Value	Average excluding the NA items	Average excluding the NA items	Average of (49, best of (58, 59, 60), 81)	Average excluding the NA items	Average excluding the NA items
Score									

WB in the table refers to the well-being enabling factors. These factors can be either conditions that support well-being— I have a friend to talk to; or an active pursuit—I worked on my hobby last week; or it can even be an attitude towards the world—I think the world is an interesting place.

While the factors themselves are elaborated in the subsequent chapters, the following table takes a quick glance at the name/theme of the well-being enabling factors.

Well-being Enabling Factors	Factor Name
WB1	Boredom and excitement
WB2	Envy
WB3	Pursuit of hobbies
WB4	Sense of purpose
WB5	Social capital
WB6	Zest

A desirable profile is when none of these scores are above 6 and if two of the scores are in the 1–2 range.

Are you surprised by your scores? If your scores are less than 6, it is good for you. And even then, you may have to reflect on how to sustain this good life. If you had a higher score, then the following chapters will help you dissect the reasons. There are several factors that may be at work. With this book, I hope you will be able to untangle them and improve your own well-being.

3

Understanding Our Sources of Stress

The Outer Theatre Factors

An entrepreneur and do-gooder spotted a lazy fellow singing and drinking by the boat at the seashore. Unable to resist the temptation, he ventured thus.

'Had you been out fishing you lazy fellow, you might be now owning a boat and a net,' he said.

'What shall I do with a boat and a net sir,' retorted the fellow.

'Don't you see this, you can catch lots of fish with your own boat and net, and besides you can rent the same to others and make more. With this you may even be able to buy a motor boat in a year.'

'What shall I do with that one sir?' the fellow repeated again.

'My Good God, with a motor boat, you can catch lots of fish, buy a truck, persuade the pharmacy in the next town to use your fish to extract cod-liver oil, export this everywhere. Within just 2 years, you will be owning a big bungalow and cars here.'

What shall I do with that one sir,' the fellow asked hesitatingly now.

'Young man, you can then come by the seashore on a beautiful evening like this, sit by the boat, sing and drink to your heart's content,' said the businessman.

'Pray sir, isn't that what I am doing now?' asked the young fellow.

The factors that cause us stress can be manifold. They can lie outside us, or inside or in their interplay. In Table 2.1, you saw how the factors that lay outside impacted your sense of well-being. They are all potential sources of stress and universal in nature. That is, by and large, any individual who has this factor in his/her external environment is sure to be experiencing this stress and coping in different ways. Since they are external, we will call it as an outer factor.

If your average score in any of the factors is >=7, you have work to do. If your average score in most of the factors are >=7, you need to make some choices soon to ameliorate the impact of these factors on your well-being.

Assessing them like we did, reflecting on them and realizing their impact on our well-being is the first step. Around each factor there is a set of social dynamics at play. The way people cope or fail to cope with each factor can provide useful insights. To a large extent, these outer stressors can elicit similar strains on our sense of well-being.

In the case studies, I have tried to portray a slice of life of normal people who could be dealing with some of these stress factors. While the stories and people are real, their identities have been masked for obvious reasons.

I wish to express my gratitude for their permission to share a slice of their life with readers for the noble cause of increasing the (readers') well-being, the primary objective of this project. Each slice of life, you would readily notice, has multiple stressors, some of them predominating the narrative. They have been positioned in the text so as to be relatable to the factors discussed. As expected, there isn't a strong one-to-one parallel between the factor and the stories shared here. This also brings home another point; it is usually the multiplicity of factors that renders us vulnerable to stress.

Family Dynamics

Immigration for work, the overall urbanization of the world, modern culture have all given rise to more nuclear families compared to joint families. The higher privacy and personal space offered by the nuclear family is sometimes also seen as an escape from stress rather than a source of stress. This is especially in the context of disagreements on the way of life between the different generations.

Prior to the arrival of children, any disruption in the mood or health of one of the partners immediately puts considerable stress on the other partner who has to now attend to the affairs of the house single-handedly. In joint family settings, this stress is much more easily absorbed by elders and other members. These additional burdens shouldered by other members in the household create some sort of a social capital and a web of reciprocity, thus building positive vibes throughout the family system. But, in a joint family, unequal distribution of labour, if it persists for long, is a source of stress.

If both members of a nuclear family work, each member may have his/her good and bad days at work. A partner often finds that the other does not give a sympathetic ear to what is being shared. If one partner does not work, then one is excessively bored while the other is excessively preoccupied, once again creating a wedge making conversation difficult.

A family dynamic where members are available to absorb the stress of each other but do not interfere in the lifestyle of its members is ideal but rare.

Parenting

While the care of children, one's own children, provides a lot of meaning, it can be a stress factor too. When they are very young, often, the needs of children have to be tended to in minutes and hours disrupting sleep patterns of adults. After the day–night rhythm sets in for children so they too sleep when adults do, it provides relief. Thereafter, the frequent infections that children become prone to are a source of stress. In a nuclear family situation, this gets aggravated as adults are ill-equipped to understand and meet the needs of (especially sick) children. Unable to understand the moodiness of children and unable to figure out whether they need to be strict or lenient, to be firm or indulgent, parents of nuclear families undergo another phase of stress. Usually, if attitude towards parenting is different between the partners, it is often a source of frequent quarrels. The underlying tone in the conflict is 'you do not trust me or you don't love the child as much as I do', understandably provoking snap reactions and conflicts.

This is one area where the presence of multiple adults in a joint family can come in handy. Elders, who have seen multiple situations, can counsel patience instead of the panic we are prone to in the nuclear family.

Here again, in a nuclear family situation and being far away from one's place of upbringing can force the new parents to make difficult choices in terms of paediatricians to go to, their trustworthiness and so on. As first-time parents, there is a learning phase to go through to figure out the relevant components of the child care ecosystem in the immigrated place.

Several groups which are commercially minded exploit the anxious parents by selling stuff that is not needed, once again inducing a sense of regret and stress in the aftermath.

As the child grows older, perennial demands for decisions in terms of school, leisure-time activities, day care all overwhelm young parents. Not only are these choices the source of stress and induce a feeling of helplessness, but even after one has made them, there is a feeling that the neighbour has got a better deal worked out giving an unverifiable gnawing feeling. As new parents, people want to ensure the best for their children and are not content with a 'good enough and fail safe' approach. This rat race in providing for children induces the same set of competition and fatigue that one experienced from young adulthood onwards and perhaps being experienced in office politics even today.

Enter the teen years, and already parents are projecting their children into the future and assessing/anticipating/fearing how things will turn out. As the child is unable to understand this background to parental behaviour, misunderstanding and conflicts develop between parents and their teenage children. Teenaged children are forming their sense of self. Often this identity is formed by making choices that are personal and unique and one that invariably leads to saying 'No' to parental requests and demands, something parents have to come to terms with.

Is All Well?

Nishita is a cheerful, well-groomed individual with a positive presence. She had the knack of creating order when confronted with a messy situation at work. She can tie many loose ends and keep the programme running. Money and recognition were the prime drivers of her professional career. What is 'uncomplicated' about Nishita is that she gives a damn to what she feels inside. They are too abstract and messy for her; she would instead seek a corresponding reality in the external world and try to sort it out. She indicates this orientation when she half-jokingly looks at FB profiles and says, 'why it is that it is always happening in someone else's life?!'

She comes from a boarding school background. This gives her the confidence to 'level with anyone'. She loves her parents and now her in-laws like any typical person, but perhaps misses the warmth and good time her mother could have given her, but for her ill health.

She sought out half-work and half-pay arrangement and added tremendous value to the several things that her team did. She almost became the right hand person of the department head, as she possessed complex data on her fingertips. Her spouse too shares the same zest for external experiences. Her only son too, at that time 6 years old, naturally carries this orientation.

Both she and her spouse led a busy lifestyle with a clear purpose to move to higher echelons of economic prosperity and comfort. A few years earlier, her son had to be operated upon, but the anaesthetist probably had overdosed him. Her son developed bouts of ill-health and there followed a dreadful phase to go through for both child and parents. Over time, he did get over it, but Nishita went through harrowing time balancing multiple priorities.

Often, under immense pressure, she would have the urge to quit work for good. It was admirable to see a woman employee balancing so much and making sure the child does not miss out on any experience. Practical tie-ups with neighbours, a technology-enabled home watch from her laptop, handling her house help with dignity, flexibility and at the same time firmness are clearly stuff everyone around could learn from Nishita. Her parents and in-laws were living elsewhere in different cities. Her network, and google, would substitute for 'what to do now?' questions that would so often confront her as a parent balancing multiple priorities.

A curious person that she is, she often talks about the progress, attitude and behaviour of her child and wonders, if all is well?

HAPPINESS MANTRA

Create a social group in the neighbourhood to lean on for resolving dilemmas about bringing up your children if you are a nuclear family. Even if this means doing business with people whom you will not interact otherwise, it is wise to have this social support. Exchange favours and extraordinary support.

Relationship Stress

Much of relationship stress is around mutuality. If you could just be yourself with your significant other and are under no pressure to conform to even subtle demands, you have a strong social relationship that can increase your immunity and keep you happy. Sometimes friends offer this social support and unconditional approval. Since we spend much of our life with our significant other, we would all like that unconditional approval in *this relationship*.

Sometimes, one can wonder if the other person is as affectionate as one is, and if the other person is as attracted to me as I am to her or him. This sense of doubt can eat into the fundamentals of the relationship.

At other times, it is the approval of others about the relationship that causes younger people to stress. When some of these doubts and worries are not even self-acknowledged but pushed down to unconscious levels because these are inconvenient realities, stress develops and manifests in different ways, making us less zestful and less present in our experiences.

Difficult Choices

Kannan is a healthy 28-year-old urban working professional at the time of this writing. He came from middle, lower-middle class economic background. To me, his parents seemed to think of him as an above the average smart child. Constraints forced him to seek work after a science degree. It was an experiment for the company to take bright science and arts graduates and that is how Kannan got into a job. He soon distinguished himself by hard work and he had a knack for quantitative stuff on tools like Microsoft excel. He also picked up his knowledge of and confidence in English as he was forced to transact with colleagues from other states. He was a solid programme assistant to a senior functionary who held a lot of power on his career growth.

Kannan wanted to do an evening MBA but permission to this was denied as it involved a few hours of break from work in the afternoons for 3 days a week. Kannan somehow sought several people's help and sought a transfer out of that team and pursued his evening MBA. He was also proving his value to the new team and was being groomed by his new skip level manager.

For a good 2.5 years, he would be teased at office because he had a girl-friend, who was perhaps in her final year of college herself. Since she belonged to upper caste vegetarian family, his colleagues would say that he has to quit non-vegetarian food. Kannan realized that the girl was too young to make any meaningful decision and counselled her to focus on her studies. 'We will marry with everyone's consent,' he would tell her.

He was also acutely aware that his caste and his social and economic status were against him. He strived in a diplomatic way to increase his economic status and one could say that he met 80% of those objectives.

When time came and the girl's father talked of planning her marriage, the news was broken and all in the family except the father eventually turned around. His senior colleagues, friends and well-wishers of both families tried to persuade the girl's father but of no avail. In a desperate situation, when it was suggested that the girl exercise her rights as an individual even if it goes against the wishes of her father, Kannan counselled the girl to not do such a thing and move on. He was fond of her and internally perhaps felt that he was taking her away from a life of better prospects. Having persuaded her, about which he felt internally good for some time, the impact of this decision on himself began to weigh in. He became a bit irregular at work, and at work too, his managers changed and he was not willing to open out his whole life to them. With the result, the new managers, though fond of his skills, found him inconsistent and began to assign his work to other colleagues.

He sought a transfer to get away from the messy situation. He became fond of biking adventures with friends, which offered a good distraction or perhaps time to be alone with his thoughts, friends who respect his privacy and fresh air.

One could say that Kannan had consciously resolved his life crisis, but subconsciously, he is yet to work out a full reconciliation of what happened and whether he took the right course and what should he do next.

HAPPINESS MANTRA

If you have to get over a bad relationship, grieve enough before you move on. Acknowledge that bad things happened to you and practice self-compassion. Imagine you are consoling a best friend going through those trials and tribulations.

Lack of Financial Predictability

In emerging markets like India, where there are lots of policy interventions and even discontinuities, a simple metric like inflation does not hold steady across the years. For example, if you earned during low inflation and when you are about to depend on your savings for living and there is a period of high inflation, then the real value of your savings are going down without yourself taking any bad decisions.

During such high inflation times, any investment of the saved capital may have 'non-performance' risks. The major spend areas also trend in unpredictable ways. Take health for instance, the healthcare costs are going up every year. Education is another area where the tuition fee and hostel fee are going up and what is even more worrisome is that there are not enough jobs for the folks passing out of higher education. This makes the investment in education a much more uncertain activity these days.

The mere uncertainty as to how much is enough for one's financial security causes misery. This leads us to feel that we must perhaps earn a little more and a little longer to secure the financial needs of our dear ones and in the absence of definitive outlook, also lets us wonder if we are spending our creative energies only earning as we are unable to estimate how much is enough.

A Dilemma

In his 40s, Sachin is a fairly cheerful and successful urban male, head of a family of 4 with 2 sons. Connecting with people and doing business with them is his signature strength. He has a constant urge to start something of his own. While young, he happily took chances that paid off. Now, with an attractive salary but certain boredom, he is not sure he should take chances again. Continuing life as it is erodes meaning for him every day but on the other side, pursuing his passion seems to be fraught with too much risk.

Or of Nethra, who is undergoing financial, relationship and parenting stressors at the same time but much more stoically. She is not sure if she is balancing the long term and short term well.

HAPPINESS MANTRA

Write down your financial plan including lifestyle expectations. Secure the bare minimum (your personal definition
of bare minimum) and make it risk-free. Mentally account
others as bonus with a risk.

Immediate or Long-term Good?

Nethra was always rated an above-average professional in her company. She had married the son of a businessman. The businessman was in real estate and about to retire, while the son worked for marketing function in a large company. Bit by the entrepreneurial bug, the son and his partner started a marketing company that would serve as a channel to sell under-construction apartments to potential buyers.

Nethra thought that this was an acceptable risk that her husband-to-be was taking. They married and they had a daughter.

When Nethra was in the maternity period, her company was running tight and attempting a 20% workforce reduction in Nethra's function. Since it was a progressive company, they were trying to accommodate Nethra by moving her to a different team. In this 5 month uncertain period, while Nethra's job role got diminished compared to her pre-maternity job role, and with her husband in business now, Nethra was trying to look for a safe haven job with equivalent job responsibility and salary.

Soon she settled into something of her liking in her own company. However, she was clear that she is not going to get a big raise that year, in fact, no one was going to. In fact, when one of her peers quit, even half of this responsibility was added to her, giving her an indication that she is not in the exit list.

An offer she pursued during the lean phase got through at this juncture. It was a small company and in fact a lesser job size. Her daughter is now 1.5 years; she said:

Prices are raising and so are school fees. Recent developments have also affected the buoyancy of the real estate market. Income from my spouse has reduced and it will take a couple of years to recover. I know what I am doing does not make sense, but I do want my child to be in a good school and not compromised on her education because of this present situation.

Try reducing your expenses, I was going to suggest. Her salary was after all 10 lakhs, not a small amount. But I refrained as it moves into personal territory. I did point out the risk that should the next job not work out, and she has to search again, it becomes hard to explain why she moved from a large to a small company and now moving out again.

I also did not know where her family members stood on this decision and if they understood all the nuances. I only knew that the sense of guilt about not providing for her daughters' education and anxiety about her spouse's income were driving this decision. In this mindset, she was not willing to reason if higher fees meant better school or few more lakhs gave her family materially more time to bounce back.

The Deadly Commute

Spending more than 45 minutes per day commuting to and from work also adds to stress. It can lead to 'eating out' if one is in a nuclear family. The members get less time to prepare food for the day as they have to factor in the longer commute. 'Eating out' in more hot and humid climes means that food is prepared at the eateries with a higher quantity of salt so as to preserve it in an edible state longer. This invariably leads to higher salt intake and makes individuals prone to hypertension.

When we don't have food in a planned manner, we tend to grab the high calorie, high salt food, once again predisposing us to several lifestyle-related diseases like diabetes.

Other than eating out, longer commute leads us to unwinding in front of the TV screen, the laptop screen and the mobile screen, thus reducing the quantity and quality of 'shut eye' we get. Lack of good quality sleep can predispose us to several lifestyle diseases, in addition to compromising our immunity levels.

In India, large-scale urban living is a 50-year-old phenomenon. Even in the Western world, it is perhaps a 100-year-old phenomenon and not older. We now work in large organizations where everyone needs to report to the same place of work. Prior to this, we were all working in small guilds or were self-employed near our place of work. Earlier to this era, adults ploughed the fields or performed other subsistent occupations all near their habitats. According to studies, longer commutes are certainly detrimental to physical and emotional health. Constant exposure to a swathe of traffic about which 'one can do nothing' engenders a feeling of helplessness.

Bertrand Russell rightly points out the other detrimental aspect of our commute. In earlier times, we hardly saw enough people on the road. Communities were more dispersed and had clear physical boundaries separating them. Except for the die-hard traveller, one often met familiar faces all of one's life. During the modern commute, we meet so many unfamiliar faces that it triggers a primitive response of assessment followed by judgement of fight of flight. This is our prehistoric brain trying to 'size up' every stranger as either a mate or prey or predator. Each time this happens, it drains away our vital energies as this is an emergency response of the body summoning all energies for this task.

It is true that for those living in the suburbs, the cost of rent and other living expenses are lower compared to the cost of living in the city which is usually our place of work. Often, we do not weigh the costs of our long commute well. If we did, many of us would be shifting closer to our place of work.

If you are living in a nuclear family, with each partner going in different directions on a long commute to work, then you surely have many sources of stress to deal with.

HAPPINESS MANTRA

Sacrifice even 10% more expenditure if you can save 1 hour of commute by moving into a different place.

24/7 Work

Thanks to smartphones and ever-connected world, we are now unable to unplug. Our body clock tells us in the morning to wind up and face the challenges of the world and as the sun sets, to wind down, reduce pace and repair our cells and organs. This logic is embedded in our biological clocks.

In this ever-connected world, we are constantly wound up, trying to catch up on work-related updates or social media-related updates and never giving ourselves the space and buffer to repair and recuperate. This 'always on' syndrome can cause nervous fatigue, suppress our immune strength and make us psychologically irritable, with the result that we just pass through life rather than enjoy it.

Without conscious cues and rituals, life can seem like one unrelenting monotonous stream of work with no escape from it. A change of clothes, a bath, a small session with your pet can all serve as cues to unwind. The 24/7 mindset removes any such cue, when we start to work through our mobile handsets and we might be doing this at home, in our beds thus giving us a sense that we have not had any breaks.

A recent study by Jean Twenge and her colleagues in *Clinical Psychological Science* points to increased suicide rates and depression symptoms amongst American youth. The iGen, as she calls for those who were born after 1995 are majorly impacted by this 'always–on' smartphone usage. Sharp increases in symptoms were reported by both the iGen and adults from 2012. The study found that as the on-screen time increased, the depressive symptoms increased. These individuals had either cut their social interactions or their sleep to be hooked onto screens.

Deadlines

The need to fight or flee danger once in a while was the lot of animals, as well as our prehistoric ancestors. Even then, it was a rare, not an everyday occurrence when you consider that we all lived in a large space like that of a forest. While the degree of anxiety in modern living is not as intense as when one's life is at stake, anxiety is now much more frequent. Every time we come under a deadline pressure, we rekindle that anxiety in smaller doses but now more frequently.

When this response system is mobilized, we go into an overdrive. In healthy, cheerful people, the system that gets us into overdrive, called the sympathetic nervous system, is well-balanced with the system that calms us, the parasympathetic nervous system.

When our parasympathetic reflexes are on, we are resting and digesting our foods, when our sympathetic system is on, we are usually fighting or fleeing. When the sympathetic system is on, the repair work of the body is interrupted, our cell oxidation rates are higher, we age faster and our internal organs wear out faster.

HAPPINESS MANTRA

Eat and sleep at the same time as much as possible. Disconnect mentally and electronically from work at least an hour before sleep time. Our work is not that important, and folks before us had infrequent connections and the sky did not fall.

Dealing with a Surfeit of Information

More choice is not necessarily good. It helps us wonder if we made the right choice at all, constantly leaving a tinge of regret in our minds. More choice and more information can lead to paralysis instead of action. Some of us in our jobs have to deal with overwhelming volumes of information and come to quick conclusions on that basis. Such are the uncertainties and changes the world is wrought with; being behind the current information sets us into thinking that we are not equipped. Take the portfolio managers for instance; their average lifespan in this job is short, usually less than 10 years. They have to constantly factor information and make or adjust their portfolios accordingly. Sure, they invest someone else's money. The fear of looking incompetent when they make poor returns on funds one has invested with them make them live on the edge all the time. Similarly, airline pilots, who have to process a lot of information in real time and react quickly, also wear out; so is the case with CEOs. The high stakes and the complexity of information processing that is required make them age faster, disproportionate to the time they have spent on their jobs. This is visible in those holding high political office. Take the case of the American President—hardly one year in office; don't you see visible signs of ageing on President Donald Trump?

More information processed is not necessarily good. It has been found in studies that those who track the stock market every hour make poorer decisions compared to those who look at it every three days. In the overwhelming swamp of immediate information, one is unable to step back and see patterns. Also, the fear that I have not looked at a piece of information, impels us to look more, instead of deciding and acting which maybe the better course with the available fund of information.

HAPPINE$$ MANTRA

Reason actively. Construct your core argument and then fill in with information. Running behind information is wasteful.

This is the story of many personal dilemmas where the surfeit of information, mostly unreliable is causing us to stress. There are instances where dealing with a surfeit of information every day under deadline pressure also stresses the individual, especially when this information becomes stale soon and once again one is on the treadmill of processing more information and within a deadline.

Fending for Himself

Arvind was the go-to person for any company performance information on its internal MIS. Right from the chairman to the CEO to many colleagues and juniors who would utilize this information reached out to him. Except for the 2 weeks during Christmas/new year, every Monday, Arvind sent a key report on company in its various internal metrics. It was almost seen as an account of 'one over' in a 50-over one-day cricket by the company's bosses.

Several of the MIS lay scattered in different systems and in an un-integrated fashion. He had to process each of them and make them fit for integration. Stakeholders for their own reasons could have defined or redefined their reports, so Arvind had to look for trends, anomalies in those trends and quickly question the appropriate individual so that he could redefine the same output in the manner he wants.

Arvind, of course, had very little authority, except to request. He was also not the type who would throw his weight around. Throwing weight are done by those who do not have stuff, was his comment to himself. He is philosophical and understanding about those refusals to provide timely information.

'They must be caught up in a thousand things of their own,' he would state over a cup of tea.

The problem was that these reports had to go exactly on the appointed hour. They were alert reports and one that could help management take timely action. This is as agile as a large company could get without disrupting operations to produce reports. The characteristic of these reports was such that their value perished over time. The following week when Arvind sends the updated report, almost everyone forgets the previous week's gem that helped take some decisive action. The urgency of the present moment would overshadow everything of the previous weeks. He often stayed up late, at least one night a week, he would be up all night and surely for couple of other half nights, he would be up, reconciling varied streams of information. He finds meaning in his work, but week after week? He was growing tired and reported the same to his manager, who understood the predicament, for he was a hands-on manager, but told him how the entire world is looking forward to these reports.

Arvind ploughed on. These were internal, so the regular accountants compiled the books in a parallel fashion. Whenever there was reconciliation, the burden of proof would fall on Arvind. Similarly, when someone was pulled up for bad performance based on this MIS, the senior executive would retaliate on Arvind and sometimes put his entire team to find some fault with Arvind's MIS. Then too, Arvind had to fend for himself, proving his truth, in a diplomatic fashion.

'Arvind is not adding value directly, he is only compiling information,' said senior managers very conveniently. They wanted this parallel MIS to stop, in their own interests. Arvind could not tolerate the meaninglessness of ploughing on, being right and being on time, all the time and then get dismissed as 'only MIS'. He sent his resignation.

Health

If one is not blessed with good health, there is an upper limit of well-being that one can reach. Tiredness, a sense of malaise or pain associated with ill-health saps away one's positivity. In sharp contrast, studies have shown that even if one lost a limb (like in a war or even an accident), happiness levels return back to near 'the set point'. This gave rise to the 'set point' theory on happiness or well-being, indicating that our sense of happiness and well-being fluctuates within a set range. Any windfall or misery produces fluctuations but we are soon into the usual range as we adapt to this new circumstance. A few months after winning a million dollars of lottery, people have returned to the same set point range of happiness before they won any lottery.

Nagging pain or sense of malaise or ill health associated with low immunity, by contrast, can diminish our happiness. We cannot rebound back as long as they are there. It, therefore, makes sense to work on our health and for policy makers to pay attention to public health. In crowded urban spaces, the concept of public health and its management becomes even more paramount because of high population density. Unfortunately, it does not receive the attention and resources it deserves. While the underlying reality of public health in our cities themselves are in pitiable condition; poor and inaccurate information about the same relayed in news channels for the sake of TRP only worsens our sense of misery.

The direct connection between stress and ill-health has been well-established by several studies. The way this mechanism operates is as follows and referred in physiology as the 'HPA' axis.

The hypothalamus (H), part of our limbic brain, produces a 'corticotrophin releasing factor', which triggers our pituitary gland (P) to produce Adrenocorticotropin hormone, which stimulates the adrenal gland (A) to produce cortisol. Higher cortisol elevates our autonomic functions such as breathing rate, pulse and blood pressure.

An elevated cortisol suppresses the repair work of the body. This suppresses our immunity.

....

The Many Tolls of External Stressors

'Positive' is how Deepa was described by her colleagues. The energy and cheer she brought to wherever she was present was palpable. Deepa was a simple-minded unmarried working executive whom you will describe as unsuitable for the politics of corporate life. Frankly, she did not care or did not care enough to trade her peace of mind. She was not exactly saintly, and she did 'bitch about' as she describes in her own words about new entrants. But her simplistic way of doing this evoked more sympathy about her naiveté then a sense of threat by the newcomers to the department.

This was the situation some years ago, but today she wanted to quit. I did get some understanding from her immediate managers but was keen to understand directly. She was in the top 10% of her peer group and anyone will hate to lose her. While her cheer continues to be high, it is not close to the levels it had been a few years ago.

The death of her dear brother in an accident had shattered her. During the phase of recovery from the bereavement, she was prone to quick tears. She became a bit disinterested. However, that did not last long, and she was back to her engaging ways. The bereavement phase seemed to have taken a toll and she was down with a form of TB, a classical compromise of immune system triggered by stress. Inexplicable tiredness characterized this phase during these spread-over several months.

She soon married and was now sad about having separated from her parents. Thankfully, her in-laws and spouse were empathetic. For Deepa, this change was not exactly unpleasant but as a change it was imposing new demands on her internal resources for adjustment. The company had selected her to go the US, and she persuaded her spouse-to-be to relocate. There were a few tense moments during this phase of planning alternatives and she did come to me for advice then. I had counselled her to decline the offer to go the US as it was not even in line with her strengths and long-term interests. This advice was taken by her reluctantly then, but now it appears right to her. This opportunity was then given to her boss.

It is during this time, she said 'whoever is my boss relocates abroad', indicating her belief in forces outside her control directing her life. Though not superstitious, she was anticipating her future with catastrophic expectations.

Her immediate provocation to quit was her recent bout of ill-health. Though the prognosis was certain cure with adequate treatment, it scared her, her parents and her spouse. Also, post marriage, her commute time will increase to 90 minutes one way.

After our meeting, we decided that the new job near home and, in fact, with a moderately higher pay is a better thing for her at this stage in life.

Difficult Boss, Office Politics and Competition

When a person in a position of authority is prejudiced against you, such a situation is also called harassment. Any efforts you put towards proving yourself have to be doubly strong compared to a person under an unprejudiced boss. One should take a distant view of such a situation and ask if there is a good return on investment in such cases, rather than a 'I will prove he/she is wrong' approach. Most human beings, including your boss are not rational beings, but rationalizing beings. They often use reason to justify themselves rather than change their mind.

Sometimes a difficult boss situation arises because of conflicting interests and the boss perceives that you are shortly going to replace him/her. In such situations, of course, you need to handle diplomatically, realize that those are going to be stressful situations and almost try to empathize with your boss who is acting to defend himself/herself.

A third situation is when your boss commands personal loyalty and alignment to his/her interests and you are not willing to give it, at least you are expressing some sort of reluctance for this personal alignment. This is a matter of your choice and the willingness to accept the consequence of that choice.

Whichever is your situation, difficult boss is indeed a source of stress, as a boss with a jaundiced eye can find lots of faults and prove them as well. First of all, you should expect it, secondly, you should hence let it not affect you and thirdly, you must build wider and formal record of your contributions. Lastly, if the organization practice and culture permit, you must seek a transfer to a different context.

Office politics can be understood as when colleagues don't exactly play by the rules in an effort to advance their self-interests. It can be often intimidating, especially for one new to work. It can take the form of bullying or ignoring or frequent put-downs or show-offs. It is important to be empathetic to where the other person is coming from, objective in assessment of threat and measured in terms of response. You must do what you must, with such a cool air that the intimidator is almost intimidated. After realizing that such tricks don't work on you, usually people reach a better compromise and clearer relationships. It does not mean that the politics will vanish, but you will know the variables and will be able to work within those idiosyncrasies.

Competition is fair play. In certain office cultures, a huge sense of competition, compared to teamwork or collaboration, is encouraged for people to bring out their best. If you are not a person who enjoys constant comparisons and races, you should avoid such culture and work contexts. If you cannot avoid them, at least develop the habit of judging yourself every 3 months instead of every day or every hour. This way, you will get a balanced view of yourself, your chances of success and your options in that situation.

Even if you are on your own, running a small business, powerful customers can act like a boss, you experience competition, sometimes fair and sometime unfair, from other players. You could benefit by applying the aforementioned very same thought processes.

HAPPINESS MANTRA

Dismount a dead horse. It is difficult to make it work, and far easier to search and settle on another live horse. This is a good mental model for thinking about your relationship with your boss.

Once you accept that these are the realities of life, the impact of these stressors will be less. However, always be aware that they do add up and we need periodic cleansing of their impact to assure our own well-being.

The slice of Rohan's life that follows illustrates some of these dynamics and as you notice, overwhelming stress is usually caused by multiple factors, not by a single factor with high negative intensity.

Resilience

Rohan comes from a family of migrants to India way back. The family migrated under adverse circumstances. They are deeply religious and even superstitious to a fault. Rohan was the younger of the two sons and considered more worldly wise in the family compared to his older sibling who is more idealistic and temperamental.

Rohan got admission into an engineering college in remote Karnataka and having completed his degree, literally came to Delhi with ₹300 in his pocket and in search of a job. His family lived and continues to live in a popular town in Uttarakhand state. He tried his hand at many businesses without an idea of what it entailed. He was a good networker and to most people appeared a trustworthy and reliable friend. He had a natural capacity to spot the needs of the person before him. The urge to help them and also believe this help was a grace of God increased his presence wherever he went.

At the same time, he often felt that there was a trouble with his health or that of his family arising out of a 'curse or similar adverse effect' that needed curing. It was not only about health; sometimes, he could feel that his family could be taking wrong decisions under the influence of this negative spell but he genuinely always believed that he himself was in his senses, all the time. He was always a willing candidate for the 'miracle cure' but when interacting with others who did not share similar beliefs, he took care not to impose it on them or judge them irreligious.

His many attempts to set up business saw him doing export-related liaisoning in Delhi. He also got into recruitment assistance and eventually into recruitment. He was a reliable person for many companies in the region fulfilling most difficult demands. He would break into a new client by simply asking for the most difficult job and create an understanding that if he cracked it, he would be given more business. Things were turning very rosy when he met with an accident. As the other person who caused the accident panicked, Rohan was able to comfort this person while he himself lay down with his legs broken. 'Just give me some water and take me to hospital.' He touched the other person's arm and got the help he so badly needed. Such was his presence and the ability to influence another person.

He recovered after a full 7 months of complete bed rest. He was also able to bounce back in his business. A few years later, another accident and he was out for 4 months and he saw in this the will of God that he must stop business.

He went to one of the firms whom he serviced as client and became an employee at much lower remuneration. This company was acquired by another and all through the turmoil, he kept his career graph rising, albeit a little slower than what he would have liked. He was not so easy to manage for his boss as he was not a typical youngster looking up to his boss.

He got on the wrong side of a powerful super boss and eventually moved out, but not before a stiff resistance. He built broad-based record of his performance, got several advocates for his contribution to the point of frustrating this very senior head. Soon he realized that his energies are better spent in a more conducive environment.

He went back to a portfolio of businesses as the corporate experience had given him some confidence to try multiple services. When he got something going, one of his employees or partners would let him down. His sense of being a perpetually blessed individual and his faith that he had higher resources gave him strength enough to fight another day, another adversity.

One of the peculiarities about Rohan that I have observed is when he has nothing to lose, he plays his best. The moment he begets success and has to defend it, the fear of loss makes him very conservative and almost inactive.

Rohan is now a moderately successful businessman, aware of the future uncertainties of his life but not quite acknowledging it to himself. He is still the resourceful, helpful friend that one can turn to and expect to be helped. He is in a dilemma between expansion and risking some capital versus consolidating and leading a good life, focusing on family and securing the children's future.

Connecting Outer and Inner Realms

We saw several external stressors and how they manifest in the lives of individuals making them prone to stress. The internal reactions to that stress are of course individual-specific. The reactions are moderated by the nature of the 'inner theatre' of the individual. They are moderated by the individuals' values and beliefs, their life positions, early life experiences and their perspectives about themselves and the world. While flavours of these reactions were present in the 'slice of life' stories shared earlier, these were particularly not focused upon. This will be the subject matter of Chapter 4. This last example will perhaps serve in making that transition.

Niraj's Choices

Niraj comes across as a bright, energetic and entrepreneurial professional, someone a boss wants as a team member and an organization would want as an employee and even a team member as a boss. His curiosity and depth of understanding and his willingness to apply have all pleased many industry stalwarts. It is hard to fathom as to when exactly Niraj turned out this way. His early education and first degree seems less spectacular, considering both his scores and the institutions he could secure admission to. From his parents, accomplished professionals themselves, he seems to have inherited a strong self-confidence and his faith in his ability to solve problems.

During his business school, he soon regretted that he did not get into a premier school; Niraj seems to have turned a new leaf at this juncture. He was determined to beat several records, one of them being the number of industry projects he would do while at school.

Niraj's overwhelming need for unique achievements is matched only by his fear that he is not balancing his books well, in terms of what he gives and what he gets. I have often noticed that just when he is about to get quite a lot, he would get impatient and would ask the other party to prove that he is valued. That has usually surprised all his seniors who could get him ahead in life. Suddenly, the transaction would become a business-like one from a visionary partnership. Once the scores are settled at this precipitation, what Niraj gets would be a pale comparison to what he could have got, had he not indulged in this premature precipitation.

The negative emotion that arises when one is taken for a ride, it seems, is too much to bear for Niraj. To me, this drove several of his bad choices. One wonders where is this streak coming from in an otherwise above-average professional in IQ, EQ, skill, knowledge, application, dedication and in practically every area of excellence one can think of. After a systematic self-reflection, Niraj is now less driven by this fear. Quite visibly, he now gets good deals commensurate with his talent and efforts.

Can you, dear reader, reflect on your own life and correlate the perspective with your scores in Table 2.1 of the last chapter, as you reflect? Does your life mirror the score patterns? Take an objective look at your life and see if there are any new items you think must be added to the list of stressors and observe how your reactions to the stressors are different from those of the characters here.

4

How Do I Know That I Am Stressed?

A King Snaps Out of Depression

There was once a king who ruled his little kingdom 1,000 years ago in India. His land enjoyed prosperity; he enjoyed security, peace, loyal subjects and many comforts. Several years into his rule, he just experienced the blues, was feeling depressed all the time, feeling listless and low on energy and drive. The queen and the ministers were understandably worried. The many affairs of the state were not being attended to. The king soon became convinced that something was wrong with him. He was desperate for a cure. Many doctors from different schools of medicine came. They checked his pulse, temperature, breathing, asked questions about any pain in the head and the tummy but could find no cause for the king's blues. When the special doctor from Iran said that the king must stop stewing in his melancholic depression, he was promptly jailed. It was then that one of his clever ministers appeared as a good doctor in search of a fortune. He said with a sombre face that the king was ill indeed and unless something is done, it is curtains! Everyone was all ears on the cure to this wretched disease.

'How many subjects are there in this kingdom?' he asked lost in his thought.

'10,000 replied the queen; including our cook's little girl that came to this world this morning.'

'Well then sir, you have a task cut out. You must go about in disguise and choose that subject who in your view is the happiest.'

'And....'

'Request that you wear his shirt for a night and return it the next morning.'

'And Sir, you can't reveal that you are the king!'

The king was finally relieved that there is a way out. He got up from his bed with a new vigour, had a sumptuous breakfast and vowed to return after completing his mission. He disguised as a merchant roaming the markets in search of some useful trade.

Each morning, he observed the fault lines of worry on every face, the farmer about his harvest, the tradesman about his business, even the children that it may rain and they won't be able to play that evening. He went to the localities that were well-off, no luck…. He searched about in places where there lived relatively less well-off people, but he could find no happy man or woman there either.

The security guard regretted he slept off that night and everything was looted. The priest was guilty that he is not giving enough good food to his children; the wife of the merchant was worried about the scar on her daughters' face and the suitor she would or would not get. Rain was threatening the potters' clay; not enough rain was threatening the paddy crop of the farmer. The steadman was worried on his ageing horse and the washer man about the drying lake.

The mission seemed impossible when the king realized, he was only to find the happiest of the lot, not one without any unhappiness. As he was walking down to his abode around dinnertime lost in planning for the next day, he heard a whistle, laughter and loud singing.

It must be the toddy with his silly fellow he thought. The notes were flawless and from inside an enclosure; he realized he had found the happiest of them all, and 'no, it is not toddy'.

'What are you having my friend?' asked the king.

'None sir, else I would have shared it with you. I will be without dinner tonight but this coconut water will serve me fine. Care for a sip?'

'Overjoyed, the king asked…might I ask you a different favour?'

'To me? I hope everything is alright with you, the poor fellow laughed at the irony.'

'Will you lend your shirt to me for the night? I promise to return it intact tomorrow,' the king blurted out his request with considerable awkwardness.

The man inside was rolling on the floor, almost possessed by a laughing fit. The king, half embarrassed and half angry bore this awkward situation when the fellow came out.

'Sorry, but I have no shirt!'

Suddenly, something 'unknotted' inside the king's mind. Ashamed, happy he walked back to the palace with a new-found purpose.

Well-being Beyond External Circumstances

The story illustrates that there is more to well-being beyond external circumstances. The king had the best of external circumstances but was stuck with the blues; the fellow who changed the king's perspective did not even have food security but was whistling with joy.

The inner life of stressed individuals could be affected with three kinds of stress proneness. They are either an anxiety about the future or grief about the past or a discomfort with present circumstance. Any of these predispositions could lead to the experience of stress. This may prevent these individuals from exhibiting an appropriate response to the external stressors. In this process, the external stressors are compounded by a poor behavioural response, leading a vicious cycle of escalating stressors.

Even while living in our palaces, we could be experiencing stress. This is because of the way we process the world. It will be over-simplistic to assume that all our troubles are inner troubles. Nevertheless, many of our troubles could be inner troubles.

Anxiety About the Future

Look at your scores in Table 2.2 for I1 to I3. Are they averaging above 6? If they are, you must certainly do something to enjoy a sense of well-being.

We are all prone to anxiety. This is the comforting news. Anxiety is part of the nature of being human. Without anxiety, we would not be taking the careful steps that would have ensured our survival. It mobilizes the whole person to be attentive and alert to avoid danger. In fact, the more anxious of our prehistoric ancestors would have survived to beget children who in-turn begot us. So, anxiety is inherent in our genes.

Studies have shown that up to seven genes may mark anxiety levels in human beings. What makes it more complicated are two other interactions of the genes. The first is with respect to early childhood experience. When childhood is traumatic and marked by intense separation anxiety from the mother, the person may have a strong imprint that the world is very unsafe. This causes a background note of anxiety in the person's mind. This would persist even if the person now lives a safe and secure life. The next factor is the present immediate environment. If the person does not have adequate social support or lives a lonely life, he/she can be prone to frequent attacks of anxiety. Where the present environment is extremely favourable, the panic/anxious behaviour get unlearnt. When the present environment is negative, the anxious behaviour gets reinforced even more firmly, worsening the symptoms and chances of recovery.

Physiologically, anxiety is associated with shortness of breath, palpitations, even some sort of pressure, pain or discomfort in the chest, a choking sensation or a sensation of being smothered, going out of control and fears of imminent doom. There are different triggers and manifestations of anxiety. Seven common ones are listed as follows.

Agoraphobia is the fear of getting into spaces and situations from which escape or quick help is difficult. Claustrophobia is the fear of closed spaces. Specific phobia is a fear of a specific object about which one has negative associations but these associations are not conscious to us. Social phobia is an attack of anxiety when about to be exposed to certain social or perfor-mance situations. Post-traumatic stress where one re-experiences the trauma. Obsessive compulsive is a high anxiety event about which one is obsessed, which is only relieved by the compulsory performance of a mitigating action. Generalized anxiety disorder is a continuous 6 months or more of anxious and worrisome thoughts.

At a milder level, anxious individuals constantly live with some fear—the fear of something going wrong in the future.

These could be thoughts about a harm that could befall us, or of harm about someone we care about. A third fear could be about us not meeting ours or society's expectation of us—the fear of falling short or failing outright.

Anxious individuals go through life's events without being fully present. They are lost in thoughts when their children are talking to them. Even while passing through beautiful surroundings, they do not notice anything but are adrift with catastrophic thoughts. Worrying about their future, they fail to live.

This is not to say that all anxiety is illegitimate. Like a good evolutionary tool, it compulsively draws your attention to the perceived danger. In the more subtle anxieties of life like the fear of catching an infectious disease, the fear of getting fired from one's job or the fear of safety of our children too, they have their legitimate place. They help us be hyper-vigilant to avoid this danger. It is only when it is carried beyond its limit into areas where one is helpless to do anything but be worried that it takes a toll on our well-being.

An anxious life makes us risk-averse. We do not pursue the new, for unfamiliar things add their own stress. This can make us less achievement-oriented, bringing us less exposure and opportunities. Some of this may then become our external stressors, again fuelling a vicious cycle of a more anxious life. We may now fear that we will fall short of expectations.

Exercises for Overcoming Anxiety

To snap out of anxiety, Dr Amit Sood recommends a beautiful exercise called joyful attention. Here, we simply start paying attention to something around us. We are asked to observe every nuance about this object. Preferably, the object should be natural, like a tree or flower, or even inanimate objects, like a table, will do. We should not be taking in many objects; just joyfully pay attention to the scratch on the table; observe its jaggedness, wonder what caused it. By externalizing our attention like this, we come out of anxious thoughts. Try it, dear reader, and observe how beautifully joyful attention gets you out of stress. Next time, try it even in adverse circumstances when you are stuck in a traffic jam. This helps us regain our balance from stress into which we descend thoughtlessly.

HAPPINESS MANTRA

Engage in joyful attention once every 4 hours in your working day. Sit down to just absorb an object in front of you. Just notice all the details, wonder what caused it, wonder how it will change tomorrow. The idea is to externalize your attention and slowly and deliberately take in the world one object at a time.

To lessen the grip of worry and anxiety on our lives more permanently, philosopher Bertrand Russell recommends an effective exercise. He asks us to write down our worries precisely without feeling awkward about it. Let us write down all the calamities that we fear might fall upon us and our near and dear ones. Let us spend 10 minutes every morning to precisely write them down. Let us also take or even initiate one action, the simplest and the best we can to secure us from this fear. After giving the devil its due, the mind will operate easy. It knows that it has not been ignored but its worries have been recorded. The following day, take a fresh page, and repeat the process. Over a fortnight, you will notice that our big book of worries is after all a dozen worries or less and repeating every day. At this fortnight, go and look up the worries about which you have not been able to initiate any action. Now picture them in all detail, as if it is coming true. By confronting this worry about which you can do nothing and picturing it so vividly, you would have become so familiar that it is not that bothersome anymore. By doing these exercises continuously, you will feel in better control of your life or at least in greater peace with it.

A similar method of getting back to our senses is recommended by the stoic Seneca. He asks us to write our worst fears and do something about them. Of the fears that we cannot do anything about, create a plan of what best I would do to make it bearable. It can be a mental resignation that such a catastrophe has indeed happened or a help that I will seek. Once this is done, he asks us to move on with life as stewing in our worries is not going to make us one inch better. As a matter of fact, if we are stewing in our worries, we may not be able to take the action that we were otherwise capable of taking. Look at his beautiful summary: 'It is ruinous for the soul to be anxious about the future and miserable in advance of misery. For such a soul will never be at rest—by longing for things to come, it will lose the ability to enjoy present things.'

HAPPINESS MANTRA

List your worries and either take action or take mitigating action or make a choice to face up to it if it happens.

A fourth method of confronting our anxieties is advocated by Rolf Dobelli, who has written about distortions in our mind and their impact on decision-making. This is called the disputation method. As we saw earlier, our inherent nature shaped by evolution magnifies our worries. If we were to statistically analyse our fears, anxieties and worries and also keep a count of how much actually came true, it will be very revealing. In the disputation method, you slow down and ask for the likelihood of the feared circumstance arising. You can dispute based on similar circumstances and the rate of such negative occurrences. If you are worried about your super boss trying to sabotage your career, you can dispute this based on if I were the super boss, would I really care? I may be more worried about my super boss and what he thinks of me rather than sabotage of the career of a skip level reportee. Usually, we will get an accurate bearing of the situation by trying to dispute our own thoughts. Such disputation is very effective when we believe that other people are going to cause us misfortune.

HAPPINESS MANTRA

Dispute the real probability of your future anxieties coming true. Find out by searching for probability of similar events.

A fifth method is to look at your book of worries and pretend it is of your close friends'. Then write down a letter of advice you would give your friend. Write about the actions he/she could take, the attitude you would advise them to have about the situation. After doing this, simply follow this advice written in this letter. When we are dealing with ourselves as third persons, our estimates of negative occurrences is accurate, and our advice more rational and we also practice self-compassion that it is alright even if this were to happen.

In summary, we can snap out of worry by paying joyful attention elsewhere or disputing the realistic chance that a worry will come true or writing them down and confronting them on the face and doing something if something can be done. After this, we must move on as our plan Bs are in place as we just advised our close friend.

The wisdom on anxiety and worry is well summarized by the writer Mark Twain. 'I am an old man and have known a great many troubles, but most of them have never happened.'

HAPPINESS MANTRA

When working through your knotty future worries or past grief or present-moment stressors, pretend you are advising your good friend who has penned them down and showing it to you. Follow your own advice to this friend.

Grief About the Past

The long shadow of the past may weigh down on your sense of well-being. There can be three kinds of grief about the past.

Bitterness is when we are unhappy with someone for what they did to us. We feel bitter when we feel let down by someone whom we trusted. We begin to feel a sense of resentment. We long for revenge. Strangely, we also blame ourselves for what happened to us, even though there may be precious little we could have done. Our conscience which informs us of the sense of right and wrong begins to admonish us for letting this happen to us. We become bitter.

Our minds produce a defence reaction to this situation in an attempt to regain normalcy. These defence mechanisms are not very conscious acts, they are subconscious. Within limits, defence mechanisms are normal and natural. It is when they get out of proportion; it causes us to distort our realistic perceptions of the world. When this state is reached, we become neurotic and in extreme instances even in need of psychiatric counselling. We defend the ego from being crushed by the overwhelming situation. The ego gets crushed from all the three sides. Society and social norms which crystallize into being our conscience are admonishing us for letting it happen to us. They may also admonish us for plotting revenge. The reality of what happened to us, which is painful, is the second side of grief. Our own biological instinct that wants to avenge the wrong that was done to us is the third side of grief. To save us from these overwhelming forces, an ego defence is employed. They may be as follows:

Repression: We remove from conscious memory thoughts relating to what is socially unacceptable. They get buried in our unconscious. They surface during night time dreaming and in some instances during day time, diminishing our ability for peak functioning.

Denial: We could be denying that the event or events happened at all or the negative consequences of the event(s).

Projection: To be able to see the world as fair, we may start believing that we invited the trouble or we caused it. We project the aggressor or the one who caused bitterness to be a victim who sought his/her revenge on us. The other alternative is to believe the world is unfair. To believe this way and work out the consequences for ourselves is harder work and hence we want to believe in comfortable half-truths.

Displacement: We could direct the revenge but unfortunately displace it and direct to another person. We may become the aggressor on an unfortunate victim. The phenomenon of student ragging is a classical displacement where the juniors begin to rag their juniors just like the way it happened to them.

Regression: We may mentally go back in time and stay there before the unfortunate event happened to us. By going back to before the event state, we are even willing to sacrifice all the growth and development we have had, just to escape the tyranny of the painful set of events.

Sublimation: We may convert this anger and bitterness to a more sublime form. For example, we may see a release of this need to avenge by indulging in competitive sports such as boxing and rugby. I am not implying that all who play boxing and rugby are playing to sublimate their need for revenge.

Some readers may feel that such reactions do not happen to them. It is good if it is not happening. In reality, studies have shown that all of us indulge in these defence mechanisms more or less. It is not apparent because it is a subconscious and not a conscious reaction. In the subsequent chapters we will show you how to scan yourself for these defence mechanisms. We will also explore how to heal from these pains and hurts without losing a sense of reality.

While we explored ego defence mechanisms in the context of bitterness, the same mechanisms obfuscate two other grief states from conscious memory and functioning.

HAPPINESS MANTRA

Before retiring to bed, recall the ego defences you employed, strive to understand why you did what you did and gently tell yourself to be conscious when you employ those defences.

They are regret and guilt.

Guilt is somewhat the mirror image of bitterness. Guilt arises in relation to other people, just like bitterness. We feel guilty when we have done something wrong or failed to do something right for those dependent on us. For example, corporate executives feel guilty that they were not available for their children during their critical moments. There are other types of conflict that produce guilt. For example, corporate executives are unable to be with their aged parents because of their career pre-occupations. While they have made the choice to pursue their careers and compromise to an extent being with their parents, this has been done without facing up to all the consequences consciously. Some consequences have been mentally denied to make this choice to defend their ego from the hardness of the choice. This produces guilt.

Sometimes guilt can be produced by acts of commission. In such instances, feelings of guilt can be very intense. It is worsened by the anxiety about being caught. The best example of this guilt and the associated mental reaction is to be found in Shakespeare's play 'Macbeth'. Lady Macbeth is crushed by a truckload of guilt and anxiety as she has aided the murder of Duncan, the king of Scotland. She indulges in repetitive, meaningless and uncontrollable behaviour—that of washing her hands. She wants to get her hands off the imaginary blood and its stink that is still there. Lord Macbeth is worried about the mental health of his wife and seeks a doctor who could cure her.

Shakespeare's words are very powerful, uttered through Lord Macbeth:

> Canst thou not minister to a mind diseased, pluck from the memory a rooted sorrow, raze out the written troubles of the brain and with some sweet oblivious antidote cleanse the stuff'd bosom of that perilous stuff which weights upon the heart.

Lord Macbeth is asking the doctor to help Lady Macbeth repress and deny, so she does not regress to the moment of crime.

Freud even goes to the extent of saying that the root of religion is guilt. That is why religious rituals have an obsessive and compulsive character about them. In psychology, this is called obsessive compulsive disorder (OCD). A person is diagnosed to be suffering from it when the urge to repeat the behaviour becomes compulsive and interferes with appropriate functioning of the individual.

HAPPINESS MANTRA

When feeling guilty, examine the source and ask if it is still valid or was it a childhood injunction carried forward unthinkingly.

Regret differs from guilt as it is about situations, things and opportunities. For example, several working executives suffer from regret for not having pursued their dream vocation. Regret arises when one is unable to resolve the conflict between the instinctual self and one's conscience, which reflects the socially appropriate behaviour. An impulsive decision or action at that point is regretted. Equally, a decision that gets taken to please authority and followed without conviction results in regret. The centre of regret is self-blame for negative outcomes.

Living in the shadow of regret prevents us from engaging with the present moment zestfully and completely. One does not want to live in the present circumstance and deny it. One is unable to switch off the mental chatter, 'what if I had done that'. The individual suffers from a sense of alienation. Alienated individuals show estrangement not only from the world but also from their own emotions.

Short-term regrets are about wrong choices made. The intensity of regret is higher if one can't do anything about it right now. Long-term regrets are about the things we did not do. The sooner one is able to convert regret into something that we can do today to reduce its negative consequence, one actually learns and grows. The moment we ruminate about regret, don't take any action and blame ourselves, we slip into depression.

HAPPINESS MANTRA

Recognize that everyone makes mistakes.

Exercises to Overcome Grief of the Past

Following are some exercises to overcome grief of the past:

Bitterness: Assertively confront the aggressor, if possible. Explain that you have moved on but wanted to let him or her know. Recognize that the person who was responsible for your bitterness is himself a vulnerable person prone to mistakes. If possible, direct a kind attention on the circumstance that led him to misbehave. Recognize that you are a victim and in no way responsible for this. Treat it like an accident.

Guilt: Recognize that everyone makes mistakes. If possible, ask for forgiveness. If your childhood has been too disciplined, realize that the fear of punishment in childhood internalizes itself as guilt. Recognize that it is immobilizing you and curtailing your full range of creative response to life. Practice self-compassion. Pretend that your best friend is going through these feelings and asking you for help. Follow your own advice to this friend.

Regret: Regret can be harnessed into personal growth by taking alternate choices now. In case it is a lost cause, imagine you are counselling your best friend experiencing this regret. What would you be saying to this friend? How would you encourage her to forgive herself? Follow your own advice to such a friend. The best way to forgive one is to ask if we are wiser by hindsight and if at that moment, one is not prone to make that wrong decision. Value the learning you got from the wrong decision and the ability to help others at that same threshold of choice.

HAPPINESS MANTRA

Be gentle on yourself when you regret, ask if we are judging too harshly from the benefit of hindsight.

Discomfort with Present Circumstance

There can also be present-moment stressors. A high score in I4–I6 in Chapter 2 is indicative of present-moment stressors. There are three such stressors.

Feeling excluded, or bullied, or being subjected to unwanted attention are the three present-moment stressors. The distinction between this and either a future anxiety or past grief is that they demand our immediate attention. Not attending to it could result in fear or anxiety about a future harm or it will soon become a past bitterness. Present-moment stressors are usually interpersonal. They are about us in the immediate environment, in the here and the now. They are not of a lingering nature as it happens in anxiety about the future or the long shadow of a grievous past.

We feel excluded when we feel ignored. The extroverts amongst us would get more agitated at being excluded. The attention and listening we get is the psychological equivalent of getting stroked physically. We may react to the pressure of exclusion with our own ego defences. We might act 'clowny' just to get everyone's attention. Or we may just withdraw into a shell and mentally resent with bitterness. When we are repeatedly excluded and if we react through withdrawal, this can lead to long-term bitterness. Acting like a clown may make us prone to take risks while withdrawal may make us over-cautious. Both are inappropriate reactions. In these defensive states, our choice-making and decision-making gets impaired.

We feel bullied when we feel belittled. The difference between exclusion and bullying is that the latter is being attended to but in an abrasive way. Exclusion is denial of any strokes, while bullying is being subjected to negative strokes. We fear our safety while resisting bullying. We become resentful when we do not protest bullying. The ego defence we could employ when being bullied is to accept the bully as a legitimate leader. This way we can deny our fears and resentment as illegitimate.

Unwanted attention is experienced more by women in our society. Men may experience it as a pre-cursor to ridicule or violence about to be unleashed. Women experience it as a precursor to harm, which can range from ridicule to rape to being the object of violence. With our increasing online lives, online stalking is a stressor of our times. Just like the extroverts amongst us can feel excluded if not engaged with, similarly the introverts amongst us may experience unwanted attention too quickly.

HAPPINESS MANTRA

Take action on a regret or value the lesson and ability to guide someone else.

Effectively Dealing with Present-moment Stressors

Where possible, increase the physical space and decrease the common time between yourself and the aggressor. Where this is difficult to achieve, increase the psychological space. We can do this by recognizing and labelling what is happening to us. We can see these acts as those of a flawed personality. Depending on our own degree of extraversion or introversion, we can engage with our surroundings.

We can also cleanse ourselves of the present-day stressors by systematically following a 24-hour cycle. In the night, before one goes to bed, recall the stressors of the day and go through your exact inner reactions. You would notice that you had repressed or denied or projected or displaced. Gently resolve to be conscious of the repression, denial and projection reactions the next time around. Even with this exercise, there would be some feelings and reactions you may deny yourself. They are likely to appear as the content of your night-time dreams in a codified form. Getting up in the morning and figuring out what your dreams are trying to tell you are a good way to unshackle the stressors. We will discuss more about this later. Also recall your body language when going through those stressors. We can subtly alter our body language to feel more equipped to deal with these stressors.

Similarly, one can start the morning by anticipating the stressful situations and people one is going to meet. We can resolve not to lose our sense of balance and resolve not to take it to heart. We can learn to practice assertiveness with the aggressor. We display assertiveness by being steadfast without seething in anger or withdrawing in protest. Assertive people verbalize their feelings clearly and without any shame. They indicate that they would live on their own terms and the aggressors' behaviour is not impacting them.

HAPPINESS MANTRA

First thing in the morning, anticipate the stressors at each hour of the day about to unfold.

Recognize that everyone makes mistakes and a little self-humour does not do any harm.

5

Do I Know
Myself Well
Enough?

We think we know ourselves. Ancient wisdom as well as modern psychology has shown this to be one big exaggeration. The motive source of our behaviour or the so-called logic of our choices is enveloped in mist. We know not why we do what we do. In fact, some distortions of our mind and reasoning are universal distortions. All men are prone to the same distortions. Through systematic experiments, behavioural economists have demonstrated that we do have in us a distorted choice-making process.

Some of our distortions are personal, not everyone has them. The distortion that Lady Macbeth experienced whenever she thought of cleanliness was personal. They arise because of our unique experiences, often from early childhood and our reactions to them.

Several human experiences are universal. Birth, being nursed or not nursed, childhood, puberty, motherhood, fatherhood, mourning attendant rituals, social sanctions and taboos (whatever they are) are universal. Our psyches, therefore, have certain common structures. But the distortions in them may be specific. Any and every such distortion stands in the way of our seeing the world accurately, truthfully.

Well-being requires seeing the world truthfully. It is about seeing it vividly, correctly, just the way it is. The stoics firmly believed that being un-deluded is being well. Just like poor eyesight can be corrected through glasses, can our distorted perspectives of reality be corrected? The answer, unfortunately, is a 'No'. We cannot have perfect 6/6 vision. We are always vulnerable to distortions. You may ask, then why bother? The good news is that we can 'minimize' these distortions. When we do get distorted as we inevitably will be, we can snap out of them faster. This is one good reason to make the effort.

How to spot the universal distortions? How to spot personal distortions? Why should we have personal distortions?

Universal Distortions

Behavioural economics examines the way we make choices. The behavioural economists contend that the human being is not a rational person as classical economists believed. The rational person would see what is right for him/her and then make the choice. After several observations and experiments, the behavioural economists have confirmed that human choice-making is flawed. The good news is that there are ways to minimize the flaws.

What is the origin of these flaws in the first place?

A short answer to this question was given by Daniel Kahneman: We have two systems by which we deal with our lives. One system that is deliberate, slow and logical in arriving at a decision and the other that is fast. The faster system is operational in us most of the time. This system is operational when we are tired or low on sugar. It is impulsive but error-prone. Subsequently, authors like Rolf Dobelli even identified 100 distortions inherent in this fast system of thinking and deciding.

Fundamentally, there are three major distortions of the fast system of thinking according to Kahneman. All the others are variations or combinations of these three fundamental distortions.

The primary distortions are (a) anchoring or priming, (b) base rate neglect and (c) loss aversion. These are cognitive distortions. Even the smartest amongst us suffer from these distortions.

Anchoring or Priming

Would you believe if I say that the decisions you took about which job offer to accept was influenced by some random pictures you happened to see 5 minutes before the decision? Would you believe that your estimation of an investment as risky or less risky was influenced by whether your toddler held or dropped the toy earlier in the day? Would you believe that your higher estimate of a certain bid was influenced by the number plate of the car standing in front of you in the signal this morning?

Am I in my senses, you may ask. What has the toddler holding a toy to do with the risk perception of an investment? Do you think one would increase the bidding price because the number plate of a random car in front of me showed a higher number?

Behavioural economists have proved that our lazy, snappy mind does not bother to think through issues. It is hard to arrive at a logical starting point for everything. In the absence of the logical starting point, the mind just starts with a random event it is able to immediately access. This random event serves to anchor the solution or decision or answer to the question in front of us. Since what serves as the anchor or starting point for our decision or estimation is random, we get different decisions depending on such arbitrary starting points. You can imagine what sort of wrong decisions this could lead to. We are anchored or primed by what just happened to us. The following experiments explain this bias in action in all of us.

In an experiment, 28 groups of 4 were assigned two different tasks. Task 1 was to rotate a roulette wheel and note down the score (0–100). Task 2 was to estimate the percentage of Amazon rain forests we have lost in the last 100 years. The only trick was that task 1 was not random but primed. 14 groups were assigned to roulette wheels that returned a number less than 20. Among the other groups, 14 had equally rigged roulette wheels that would return a number greater than 80.

When they went to task 2, an independent factual and rational question, an interesting thing happened. The first set of groups who had a number less than 20 in the first task, estimated the loss of rain forests to be close to 37%. The second set of groups that had a number greater than 80 in the first task estimated the answer to the same question to be about 66%. Surely, the first task should not have influenced the answer to a second independent question. Unfortunately, when the groups worked on the second estimate, they somehow started with a less than 20 or a more than 80 number and kept adjusting the answer based on factors they knew. This is a wholly irrational approach to link a roulette wheel outcome to a specific question on loss of rain forests. They had no connection, but affected by priming. This arbitrary initial point for the groups distorted their estimation.

Consider another experiment where students of a college were asked to do 'free association'. Free association is an exercise where a word is given to you and then you are required to keep on uttering words that come to you without bothering about their logical connection. The experimenter randomly divided the class into two groups and assigned the first group harsh and intense words as the trigger and the second one mild or light words. The first group had blood, revenge, war, anger and such like words, while the latter group had words such as flower, soft, affection and friendship. Considering the experiment over, the student volunteers handed over their papers to the experimenter and walked out. The experiment was not over. A set of people were timing the speed with which the student volunteers walked a long corridor before they got down and went their own ways. The group with the more intense words clearly walked faster compared to the group with the milder trigger words. Why should the pace of our walking depend on a random free association task we completed minutes earlier?

A third experiment: Unlike in India, in the US, offices have unmanned counters for small snacks. They are usually open and those who want snacks need to pick them up and drop the relevant money into a drop box. Culturally, it is considered rude to take up snack and not drop the money or drop a lesser amount. However, as you would expect, often the value of snack that vanished will be more than the money deposited. This is when they put the picture of a face with prominent eyes in front of the counter. Voila! Now more money was deposited for the same snack consumed. The experimenters were now unsure. They then removed the picture and the money deposited reduced. They now put the picture on Thursdays and only Thursday had higher contribution compared to snacks taken. What is in an inanimate picture? Why should it make the employees honest?

Our minds are associative. They are not logical, especially when the fast mode is on.

Overcoming Anchoring or Priming

It is useful to deliberately search and remove the impact of priming in our decision-making. Take a moment to recall a potential priming event. Try and imagine that an opposite event has happened recently, and proceed to come up with a second answer. Examine the variation between the two answers.

For example, in the snacks experiment, the opposite of a 'watching face' image is to imagine the room is dark.

Have you noticed people ordering the same food they see served in the next table? This is a priming effect. Wait a few moments longer and see other food being served as well before you make a choice. Sometimes, it is even useful to strike the first food you saw being served off the choice list, unless that dish is a popular one at that restaurant.

Further, if you are on an empty stomach and notice you are being primed with certain stimuli, postpone the decision.

HAPPINESS MANTRA

Look for a priming event around your next decision. Do imagine an opposite event happened; would your decision have been any different? Do weigh both the decisions before plunging ahead.

Base Rate Neglect

Neglecting the base rate of an event is another big distortion plaguing our decision-making and anxiety. Base rate neglecting is misestimating the frequency of occurrence of an event. We are unable to distinguish between the intensity of an event and the probability (rate or frequency) of its occurrence. Most of the people intuitively feel that train travel is safer than air travel. This misperception occurs because there are no air crash survivors but there are train accident survivors. This does not imply that air crashes are more frequent compared to train accidents. In fact, the opposite is true. For every one lakh journeys, the number of air crashes is far fewer than the number of train accidents.

In an anxious situation, we overestimate the incidence of a negative event. When we are worried about our child's health, a headache may suggest the possibility of dengue fever. Even though a dengue is a much less likely event compared to a sinus, that is, having a low base rate, it is our anxiety that is distorting us to misestimate the probability of dengue. We are additionally primed by TV channels on the incidence of dengue. We are after all the descendants of paranoid ancestors. Being paranoid had a survival value in the past. It was better to think that the moving shadow is a predator and be proven wrong. It would have been deadly to think it is a cloud and get eaten by a predator. It is our paranoid ancestors who survived to procreate. Paranoia and anxiety are hence part of our genetic constitution.

When our head has dull and persistent pain, we imagine tumour, although it is a rare occurrence. This is an example of our anxiety overshadowing reason. We neglect the fact that tumour has a small probability because it is an intensely negative event.

This anxiety can reach dysfunctional levels making us freeze in fear.

Similarly, unfounded hope also springs because of base rate neglect. When a guru or self-help author promises miracles and cites illustrative cases, we fail to ask a few questions. We don't ask if there are individuals who practised it and still failed. We also don't ask if those who did the opposite of what the guru recommended succeeded and if so, what explains their success. Since the examples given by the author are handy, and our lazy and snappy selves won't bother to check the counter-examples, we are led astray. This is also called survivorship bias or adverse selection bias. The successful companies who followed the management guru's advice are alive to tell the tale. The companies who followed the advice but perished are not even present. They may even be more in number compared to the successful companies!

There is after all wisdom in the maxim, 'Dead men don't tell any tales.'

Some of these erroneous beliefs can be dangerous. You only have to look at the number of people who sought miracle cure for their cancer and postponed critical treatments. They eventually came to grief.

HAPPINESS MANTRA

Next time your own belief or someone's prognosis is making you anxious, pause. Find out the evidence presented for the opposite of this to come true. If there is none presented, relax. Most probably your concern is overstated. For example, if an authority figure says, 'if you do, you will be damned...', ask for or seek evidence of people who did and were damned and those who did not and were still damned. Similarly, if an authority figure says 'If you didn't, you will be damned...', ask for or seek evidence of those who did not and were not damned and those who did and were still damned.

Overcoming Base Rate Neglect

A good way out of the base rate neglect is to follow a three-step process before believing in something. The first step is to consider the opposite of our belief. The second step is to ask what evidence is needed to prove the opposite of our belief. The third step is to ask what information is provided by the guru or self-help author with regards to this evidence. If they do provide comprehensive evidence, then believe in it. If they don't, become suspicious and look around for this information yourself.

Loss Aversion

This is the third primary cognitive distortion. In fact, this one has emotional characteristics also.

Gains make us feel good, but losses don't make us feel bad, but miserable. This is loss aversion. There is the inherent aversion to loss in all of us. If we had to play a game where the chance of winning ₹2,000 is 50% and the chance of losing ₹1,000 in the game is also 50%, most of us won't play such a game. Even if we lost the first game and the second and third, if the probabilities are true, we will soon reverse our misfortunes. In the long run, we will be better off than worse off.

Perhaps, the scarcity that was the lot of our primitive ancestors gave rise to this distortion. 'A bird in hand is worth two in the bush' is a saying perhaps born out of the loss aversion tendency.

Loss aversion can lead to suboptimal decisions and outcomes.

In an interesting study, two groups of students were given the following intervention. In the first group, the teachers praised them for being smart. In the second group, teachers praised them for putting in good efforts. The traditional belief of the psychologists was that the first group will develop a better self-image. They will believe in themselves, become more confident and do well. Instead, something else happened. The group was obsessed about their smart label. They feared that if they tried something adventurous, they would fail and lose this smart tag. They stopped trying to solve difficult problems as there was a possibility of failing and thereby damaging their image. They became extremely loss averse. Over time, it slowed down their growth, development and mastery of the material. The group that was praised for putting in right efforts had no such loss aversion. The very thing they were praised for was within their control. They went on to put even more efforts, became adventurous, attempted the more difficult problems and grew.

The same phenomenon happens when we buy a portfolio of stocks. If one of these stocks suffers a loss and another stock gains such that the net value of the portfolio remains unchanged, we will still remain unhappy—because as soon as something becomes ours, we attach a higher value to the same object. We cannot bear to lose it. We become irrationally invested in the object we have just acquired.

The Economics Nobel Laureate Richard Thaler demonstrated this in his class. He randomly distributed a coffee mug to half his students. After sometime, he started a market for these coffee mugs. Since the distribution was random, he expected half of those who have the cups, that is, a quarter of the whole class, to sell and half of those who did not get the cups, again a quarter of the whole class, to want to buy. The students were free to put a price for the sale. Those who had the mugs would not sell for less than $5.25 on an average and those who wanted to buy would not want to give more than $2.25 on an average. As soon as they possessed the mugs, the students had become irrationally invested in it. Their asking price to sell became unreasonably high.

Loss aversion is the reason why we do not clean our closet of the things we don't need anymore. It is the reason why we overprice our houses when we want to sell them. We often find no buyer and eventually lose more as an earlier sale would have earned us interest.

Overcoming Loss Aversion

The simplest way to overcome loss aversion is to re-imagine it as a gain for which you are spending efforts. Imagine the object did not belong to you and you are trying to acquire it. What price would you pay for acquiring it? The price can be monetary or it can be psychological or physical effort.

Are you considering moving closer to your workplace to avoid commute? If you consider this as giving up your larger house and going to a smaller house to avoid the commute, you would probably not make the decision. If you imagined that you have come to the city and are considering living in a big house but away from work versus a smaller house closer to work, you are far more likely to make the decision that is right for you.

If the stock you purchased is not doing well, it is wise to put a limit to the amount of loss you will tolerate on it. For example, if you purchased a stock for ₹1,000 and it is trading at ₹800, you can mentally decide that should the stock fall to ₹750, you are going to sell it and limit your losses to ₹250 per stock. Instead, investors find it hard to admit that they have suffered losses. They persist and sometimes even pick up more of the stock at ₹800. They will buy another 'X' quantity of the stock at ₹800. They think that the average cost of the stock is now ₹900 (i.e., average of ₹1,000 and ₹800) and they will make profit the moment the stock bounces back to ₹950. Just because they have the stock, they become over-invested in it, just like Thaler's students. Most often than not, they increase their losses as their stocks fall even further.

The wise course of action would be to put a limit or stop the extent of losses. Since this could be hard to imagine, you can look at it as an advice to your close friend. Would you advice your friend to buy the stock now at this reduced price? If not, promptly sell yours as you could be the victim of loss aversion and on way to making a bad decision.

HAPPINESS MANTRA

Re-imagine the 'fear of loss' in your next decision as 'greed for gain'. If this item I fear I would lose had not been there with me in the first place, would I bid for acquiring it? If the answer is no, you are overstating the importance of this loss to you and lying frozen without being enterprising.

Some Combination Distortions: The Choice Architecture

The phenomenon of choice architecture in decision-making is a classical combination distortion. Priming, loss aversion and base rate neglect are visible when we consider decisions we make under a pre-fixed framework. Often this framework is innocuously suggested to us with a view to manipulate us to make a bad choice.

If you have recently shopped for a car, you would relate to this readily. You will notice that there are three versions to the model you have selected. First is the base version, say at ₹7.2 lakhs on-road price. The second would be a standard version at ₹7.7 lakhs which would have a lot more features such as power windows, better upholstery and so on. The third would be a premium version at ₹8.2 lakhs but which will have trivial features such as speaker, leather panel and wooden finish. The third version is the decoy. It is obviously not value for price. You would tell yourself that the standard version for the price has several critical features while the premium version is too high for the incremental features. This is the idea of the car sales dealer. You may only need the base version. He has primed you by showing the other costly version against which the standard appears most reasonable. He has also provoked a loss aversion where you feel relief on avoiding the loss from the premier version.

The net result is that the base version is perhaps the right decision for you. By subjecting you to these distortions, the car sales dealer made you choose the standard version. Most surprisingly, you felt good about choosing the standard version.

This is the same reason your coffee comes in three cup sizes. You often chose the middle size when you actually need the smaller version. The cost of acquiring another customer is steep for the coffee shop, so he shows three sizes and tempts you to the middle or even the large cup. You will notice that the size 2 prices are not two times the size 1 price and same with size 3. The incremental coffee comes cheaper for you, sure. The sales cost of selling the incremental coffee is even steeper for the coffee shop owner. He has had the better deal in the bargain, whereas you have consumed additional quantities of coffee that you did not intend to have in the first place.

The same happens with one scoop, two scoops or three scoops of ice cream proposition.

Even smart people are not immune to the choice architecture. Consider the choices made by the readers of *The Economist*. In the first campaign, the newspaper/magazine gave three options for buying or renewing:

Option 1—Web Subscription ($59) One year subscription to Economist.com includes online access to all articles from *The Economist* since 1997.

Option 2—Print Subscription ($125): One year subscription to the print edition of *The Economist*.

Option 3—Print and Web Subscription ($125): One year subscription to the print edition of *The Economist* + online access to all articles from *The Economist* since 1997.

Guess what: Option 2 is evidently inferior to option 3, so amongst readers, 16% went for option 1, 0% for option 2 and 84% for option 3.

Enter the second campaign where only two options were given:

Option 1—Web Subscription ($59): one year subscription to Economist.com includes online access to all articles from *The Economist* since 1997.

Option 2—Print and Web Subscription ($125): One year subscription to the print edition of *The Economist* includes online access to all articles from *The Economist* since 1997.

Something dramatically different happened in the second campaign. Notice that the choice architecture and choice sets were different in the second campaign. Out of all, 68% went for Option 1—the web subscription, and only 32% went for Option 2—the print and web subscription.

The seller is playing on your loss aversion and priming effects to sell you something for $125, whereas you would have bought an equally good alternative for $59.

Overcoming Choice Architecture

Eliminate the middle option. The middle option which is close to the first or third option is a decoy to lure you into buying what you don't want. Reconsider your decision after eliminating the middle option.

HAPPINESS MANTRA

When three options are presented to you, eliminate the middle option (imagine it did not exist) and see which one of the other two you truly want. Go with this choice.

Mental Accounting

Partly a priming effect, we attach different levels of importance to the same value of money depending on how we earned it. If we had won money in a lottery, we are not averse to spending it casually. Money hard earned is spent very conservatively. As an individual, I may have earned some of my money easily and some of it the hard way, but spending habits should not be dependent on this. As we saw repeatedly earlier, we are not rational in our choices. This is another mental distortion.

Instead of being a victim of mental accounting, the stoics actually used it as an advantage. They used an exercise called mental subtraction. Dobelli has the following powerful exercise to illustrate the power of mental subtraction.

Could you imagine that you no longer have one arm (don't look yet), then a few more breaths later, even the other arm. What you have is only a short stump of muscle on either side. Imagine how you are going to navigate the world. How are you going to eat, hug your child, cycle, pick up your favourite magazine? Close your eyes if it helps to bring vividness to your imagination. This little exercise has boosted the sense of well-being of individuals.

The stoics kissed their children wishing them well and then almost muttering that this could be their last day. Some philosophers used to sleep on a coffin-like bed, signifying that they are already dead. When they do get up the next morning, whatever follows is felt as nothing but a gift. By thus imagining they had lost objects and experiences that have hitherto belonged to them and rediscovering them in their possession, many people have boosted their sense of well-being. The experiences and objects are now counted as blessings. The exercise of mental subtraction has been proven to be far more amplified and long-lasting than even the exercises of feeling grateful to others.

HAPPINESS MANTRA

Use 'mental subtraction' every day to feel good. Imagine you have lost those possessions and imagine how you will operate. You may picture the difficulty of doing things that you have taken for granted. Now discover them in your possession and you will boost your sense of well-being tremendously.

It turns out that our mental accounting of pleasure and pain is flawed too. Like the two systems of thinking—a fast, snappy and lazy system versus the slow, deliberate and logical system. Kahneman discovered there are two separate processes of memory creation, storing and monitoring.

The first one he called the experiencing self. It is flawed to the extent that it forgets most of its experiences. The experiencing self lives in the here and now. It takes in experiences in spans of approximately 3 seconds each, stores a few and discards many of these moments.

The second one he called the remembering self. This is the photo album of our lives. It is flawed to the extent that it distorts the pleasure or pain depending on two factors as the following experiment showed.

Volunteers in the experiment had to dip their hand in 14 °C of cold water for a full one minute. They found the whole experience unpleasant. In the second instance, the volunteers had to dip their hand in 14 °C of cold water for a minute and then in 15 °C of cold water for a further 30 seconds. A day later volunteers were asked which of the two experiments they would like to repeat again: A large number of people opted for the second experiment. Objectively, the second experiment entailed greater suffering. It had the same 1 minute of dipping in 14 °C of cold water plus an additional 30 seconds in 15 °C of cold water. 15 °C of cold water is by no means a pleasant experience. However, participants preferred the latter because the peak suffering was similar but the ending was better even though the duration of torture was longer. Daniel Kahneman has named it as the peak-end rule.

Kahneman advises that if you had ₹50,000 for your vacation, it is best to take three short vacations rather than one long vacation. He points out that after 2 days of vacationing, the mind will get used to the better climate and scenery and will no longer get the same pleasure though the money spent per day will be the same. The same money and the same amount of time will yield more pleasure if spent on a different vacation trip. Further, a few months later, the length of the vacation will not register as pleasurable when you recall. Recalling three separate vacations in our memory store will give more pleasure in the aggregate.

HAPPINESS MANTRA

Use the 'peak-end' rule to increase the sense of well-being for yourself as well as for those with whom you collaborate at work, home or hobby club.

'Focusing' and 'End of History Illusion'

Imagine playing with our favourite toys as little children and then one that we were trying to grasp just being snatched away. We would have howled and behaved as if the world was coming to an end. Now imagine another version: We had done with the first toy, we gently turned to another toy, and the one we were playing with 5 minutes ago is now taken away. Most of us would not even notice it, forget about missing it. We bring pretty much the same attitude to whatever we are focusing on. Somehow it seems to be life and death for us. This mental distortion is a combination of base rate neglect and loss aversion. Daniel Kahneman sums it up very nicely, 'Nothing in life is as important as you think it is while you are thinking about it.' When we focus too much, we misread the intensity of the event and the probability of the event. We read them both as high.

A related illusion is the end of history. We strongly believe that we have made up our mind on what we want. We won't change or evolve from here on. Dobelli asked people how much they have changed in the last 20 years, on a scale of 1 to 10, from 1 (not at all) to 10 (drastically). Most people gave themselves a number between 2 and 4. When the same question was posed about the next 20 years, that is, how much they believe they will change, the answer was a score between 0 and 1. Psychologist Gilbert posed this question not about personality and values but about preferences. He asked people, 'What was your favourite band 10 years ago?' and 'How much you will pay to listen to them today?' He then followed up with, 'How much will you pay to listen to your current favourite band 10 years hence?' Despite the obvious relatedness of the two questions, people were willing to pay 60% higher for their current favourite band 10 years later compared to their past favourite band today.

The take away from both these illusions is that our preferences change rapidly and will do so in future as well. By focusing without perspective and fretting about losses, we are not going to lead a good life. Bertrand Russell beautifully sums up the recipe for the conquest of happiness by saying that one must have 'varied impersonal interests.' And, to believe that one's work is terribly important is the starting point for nervous breakdown. How true!

HAPPINESS MANTRA

Ask yourself now and then: Will I even remember what I am fretting about today, 10 years from now? If the answer is no, relax, the outcome of what is happening is not terribly important.

Personal Distortions

Universal distortions are mostly cognitive save some like loss aversion which also had an emotional undertone. The personal distortions that arise from our psyche are more emotional. These emotional undertones drive an inappropriate engagement with our world. To find out why they occur, we must understand our psyches. Our psyches distort the world for us. How and why they do this distortion? What are the contents of the psyche? How do we acquire one? Psychoanalysis deals with these intriguing questions.

Freudian School

Freud is the founding father of psychoanalysis. Freud analysed the psyche as composed of the id, the ego and the superego. The id is our instinctual self. It is what we would do if there were no restrictions on our functioning. We will follow the pleasure principle, that is, seek pleasure and avoid pain. The superego can be loosely described as our conscience. It gives us a sense of right and wrong. Our superegos are usually formed around our parental image. The ego is sandwiched between the superego and the id. It takes a pragmatic view of things. It operates on the reality principle.

Early childhood experiences have an important bearing on the formation of our ego and the superego. As little children, our identity or sense of self was vis-à-vis the world. We recognize the mothers' breast as the first object outside of ourselves and a source of pleasure and nourishment. From this first object slowly we realize that the world outside is different from the self inside. And, the world is indifferent to our will and pleasure. We begin to cajole and manipulate the world to do our bidding and, depending on the response we receive from such bidding and cajoling, develop notions about the world at large.

Our parents or parent surrogates are the authority figures for us. They can give or withhold what we want. To give us what we want, they impose a set of dos and don'ts. Several of these dos and don'ts are for our safety and well-being but as children we are not in a position to appreciate it. We only internalize that we need to abide by some dos and some don'ts. This is the seed for our superego—our internal censor that accepts certain actions and thoughts and inhibits and experiences repulsion against other actions and thoughts. We resent and rebel against this discipline and at the same time welcome the certainty and security it provides. We become ambivalent to our parents and parent-surrogates and also ambivalent to our own superegos. We dislike our superegos but cannot live without it either.

For some individuals, childhood had been spent in a safe or nourishing environment but for others in an indifferent or even violent one. Then ego concludes that the world is not safe or reliable. It gives rise to chronic anxiety. This original anxiety which one internalizes from an abnormal childhood persists long after the environment has turned safe. Several mental illnesses can be traced back to such extreme childhood experiences.

As we grow up, even after a normal childhood, we are unable to resolve this ambivalence towards parents and other controlling authority figures. When we are able to move and grasp, we try to seek pleasure. The ego is now caught between the pleasure that the id is forcing it to seek and the admonition of the superego which is against it. This ambivalence and conflict is too much to handle. The ego pushes these thoughts down.

Now and then, a thought considered inappropriate by society and the superego bubbles to the surface. The superego censors the thought and it gets repressed. Repression is unconscious suppression. It is not consciously evaluated and disposed. The dismissal happens even as the thought arises, almost instantaneously, in a tearing hurry—without the ego becoming fully aware it. This banishment leaves the ego a bit uneasy, but all the same the ego resumes its engagement with the world. These repressed thoughts are further linked to other such similar earlier experiences. They become buried deep inside and unconscious. These buried repressed thoughts' accumulating in the unconscious region of our psyche is source of our personal distortions.

The discovery of the unconscious was one of the greatest contributions of Freud. The unconscious harbours our secret desires, hopes, wishes, fears and anxieties. It is a deep ocean. Freud likened our consciousness to the tip of an iceberg, just a tenth of it above water whereas the rest of the iceberg, about 9/10th is buried under water. One can imagine that this large and powerful unconscious has a strong hold on the way we lead life and our sense of well-being. It is hard to access the unconscious directly because the ego cannot handle its contents. By a systematic process called psychoanalysis, the impact of our unconscious selves on our life can be better understood and managed.

A lot of the chatter in our inner theatre and in our stress profiles is unconscious in origin. To get well, we have to uncover, accept and, if possible, sort and neutralize its deleterious contents.

The growth and development of every human being conforms to a universal, unfolding (epigenetic) structure. There is the pain of birth, the sensory onslaught of the world at birth, the problem of obtaining nourishment, digestion, helplessness, locomotion, injunctions of dos and don'ts, language, communication and associated socialization. This typical structure gives rise to a corresponding structure in the individual human psyche.

Since the dawn of civilization, these very activities have also made for the formation of a broad common social structure in human settlements. What exactly happened to us and how we responded to it within this broad context have resulted in our specific unconscious material. All individuals go through certain common developmental (epigenetic) stages; each of these stages obliges every individual to negotiate and resolve one way or the other certain existential dilemmas which are also, paradoxically, universal. In the course of its phylogenetic history, the human race has generated and accumulated a number of myths which are found across regions, cultures and languages—even when there had been no contact among them. Each of these myths crystallizes an intra-psychic conflict and also a way of resolving it.

Psychoanalysis points out that myths correspond to certain complexes that are precipitated as we negotiate the epigenetic stages of development. Myths can be used to interpret and understand individual developmental crises and resolve them. They are timeless models offering eternal signposts on the pathway to well-being.

The idea is to know oneself one step more deeply than what rational reflection can reveal: Psychoanalysis can help here because 'psychoanalysis is the science of the irrational'. By accepting the irrational part of ourselves honestly, we can achieve higher psychological integration between our conscious self and unconscious self. Such integration will mitigate the free floating anxiety haunting our being. Free association, dream analysis, projective story-telling, analysis of inadvertencies, autobiography are several inexpensive psychoanalytic techniques and methods that can be adopted to know oneself deeply.

Transactional Analysis

TA, as it is popularly called, is also a study of human psychology. Like Freud, the transactional analysts, also hypothesized that there seems to be three different people inside every person. They called them 'ego states'. At any point, one of them is dominant and reacts to the world. The personality of a person or the pattern of his/her behaviour is determined by ego states he/she deploys against different external situations.

The three ego states conceptualized by the TA school are the 'parent ego state', the 'adult ego state' and the 'child ego state'. The transactional analysts used more colloquial vocabulary so that their discipline can more readily and widely spread. They further characterize the parent ego state into two sub-states—the 'nurturant parent' and the 'critical parent'. Similarly they characterize the child ego state into three sub-states—the 'adaptive child', the 'little professor' and the 'natural child'.

The TA school felt that analysing an individual in the abstract is less helpful. It is better to understand the individual through his/her interactions with others. When these transactions are analysed, we understand what is driving a person. This is how this discipline got its name—transactional analysis.

The parent ego state is the moral principle—roughly, the superego; the adult ego state is the equivalent of Freud's reality principle while the child ego state is the equivalent of the pleasure principle. In the adult ego state, we assess and test reality and solve problems. However, this ego state does not have any inherent preferences. It lacks emotional valence. The star trek character 'Mr Spock' is a personification of the adult ego state. He was cold, logical but cannot set any goal or pursue things for their own sake.

The parent ego state is the 'internalization' of the different injunctions we received in childhood. We 'play-act' the same on others in our transactions. We can be perceived as critical or disapproving of other people's stances or actions when we are operating as a 'critical parent'. We can also be the source of encouragement and approval when we operate as a 'nurturing parent'. A stronger internalization of the dos and don'ts at childhood results in a parent-ego-dominated personality.

The child ego state is the other end of this spectrum. This represents our typical reactions to these injunctions as also our original wish to be spontaneous and un-encumbered. As we saw just a while ago there are three sub-states to the child ego state. They are the little professor, the adaptive child and the free child. The child that manipulates the parent and social norms and tries to peer behind them to get what it wants is the little professor. The child that conforms to these very norms to obtain security and approval is the adaptive child. The child that wishes to remain spontaneous and un-encumbered is the free child or spontaneous child or natural child.

The third ego state is the adult ego state. It does not have sub-states. It represents our problem-solving, estimating, reality testing selves.

Rituals, Past-times, Games and Scripts

What to do with one's time is a burdensome question for the individual according to the transactional analysts. The conflicting claims of our ego states tear our persona in different directions. Instead of uncovering, confronting and resolving these, most of us resort to pre-programmed transactions. According to the TA, it is not the mentally ill but even the so-called normal people who indulge in pre-programmed transactions all the time. It saves them the burden of making choices and accepting consequences. We slip into ready-made modes rather than make a choice anew on what to do with our time. The goal of TA was to help individuals lead a programme-free existence where you would follow your own music rather than dance to others' tunes.

It is to avoid the structuring of time (what to do with our time?) that ritual and pastimes were invented. Rituals allow strangers (and we are all strangers to each other!) to interact without getting intimate. We can safely perform our end of the ritual without having to understand the other person or offer intimacy which may make us vulnerable, even though it makes us free. This is why rituals pervade every sphere of human life. The meeting ritual, the greeting ritual, the rituals around birth, puberty and death are all conventions to structure time and let us be inauthentic, without feeling guilty about it.

Pastimes are similar to rituals. Small talk is a pastime. They are not structured like a ritual around transitions and occasions. Nevertheless, they too are inauthentic transactions. For example, you talk about the weather when you want to talk about something else.

Games are pre-programmed transactions between people. When people with certain personalities interact, they will always transact to a predictable outcome. The context and content of their transaction is merely a stage to enact the pre-programmed drama. For example, a spouse who quit or scaled down her career to take care of the family may resort to a gamy transaction whose core message is 'If it weren't for you'. Similarly, some of us who almost take pride in being beset with insolvable problems will resist help. Taking help and solving the problem will make our lives vacuous as there is nothing else to do with our time. These individuals always have a core transaction with their helpers which runs as follows. The helper offers a suggestion, 'Why don't you....' But the person refuses it subtly by saying, 'Yes, but....' What gets filled in the '...' is merely incidental. The helper and the helped are bent upon indulging in this transaction with a pre-programmed outcome of 'this person is incorrigible/ my problems are complex and unsolvable'. The helper is equally at fault in engaging in this game. 'Boys are stupid', 'See what you made me do' and several such gamy behaviours have been analysed in this approach to analysing interpersonal transactions.

Scripts are subconscious story lines we have decided to enact. Eric Berne, the father of TA goes to the extent of saying that all our major life decisions are taken by this script. To quote him, 'where will we work, whom we will marry and who will be near our deathbed are all pre-decided' by us in this script. Script is not presented like fate over which we have no control—whether by a powerful God or random chance. This is the subconscious truth about ourselves that we have decided to believe in and are acting out our lives according to this belief. Berne and latter experts synthesized about 6 major life-scripts—core stories around which lives are enacted.

TA gives another pathway to well-being: Observe our own transactions and uncover our predominant ego states, our rituals, pastimes, games and scripts and thus uncover a lot about ourselves. A deep analysis followed by a light vigilance during the day and end-of-day review and reflection of our transactions will create an intimate personal understanding.

HAPPINESS MANTRA

An analysis of your own transactions last week will give you the games you played, the predominant ego states that surfaced in you and the inauthentic rituals and pastimes you indulged in. With this understanding and vigilance, at the next instance, resist your temptation and break the pattern. If you feel good when you broke the pattern, do more of it.

6

My Working Self: A Personalized Analysis

External and internal factors diminish well-being; however, letting this happen or not is very much in our hands. But for that, we need to have a greater understanding of our self. Through the prism of universal distortions, we obtain a general understanding of ourselves. A personal understanding is obtained by systematic self-analysis, and self-analysis is not easy. The subject that is analysing is also the object that is analysed. Analysis itself is subject to distortion. We could get primed or anchored in our analysis, could misestimate the breadth and depth of the issues or present our own distorted versions of our stories. We have repressed/pushed down and stowed away certain experiences from the reach of our awareness because they had been too painful to face squarely. Since they have never ever been there in the full light of our awareness, they cannot come on their own. We have drawn an invisible curtain on these experiences and it is difficult to remove the invisible curtain by normal methods of introspection (self-inspection).

Creating a personalized private space to record incidents and feelings of our day-to-day life will facilitate self-analysis. There are inexpensive but powerful analytical tools for a deep scan of our self.

TA and error analysis are good tools for the beginners of self-analysis. They point to the root of our distortions so we may uproot them. The roots of our distortions lie hidden in the dark corners of our psyche.

In TA, we learn to identify dysfunctional patterns in our transactions. These patterns reveal a hidden but firm position we have taken about ourselves and the world. These positions often distort. Every transaction subject to an analysis is good material for this personalized scan of our waking self, our working self.

Our errors, omissions and temporary forgetfulness are rich sources of data too. They are harder for us to recall but easier to observe in ourselves and others. They reveal a lot about things we want to omit, forget and misplace. They are our unconscious directing us in surprising ways.

Once these two are mastered, we can utilize our dreams in the night to peer into further depths of our psyche.

How can transactions with others reveal personal distortions about us? Is there any more to transactions we have with others?

Why and How We Transact?

Since all of us are made of ego states—the little people within ourselves with their quirks—transactions are about interactions between the little people inside us with the little people inside others. Our parent (nurturant or critical), our child (spontaneous, adaptive or little professor) or our adult ego states are the ones which are interacting when we interact. These interactions could be rituals, pastimes, games and scripts. But why indulge in the transactions?

Eric Berne, the father of TA, introduced the concept of hunger to shed light on this matter. We need to satiate our hunger for food. This is obvious. We also need to satiate our hunger for stimuli, recognition and structure.

In human growth and development, food hunger is the prime mover in the toddler years. The mother responds to it by nursing and care-giving. Every nursing episode is followed by separation from the mother. How will the child now seek the equivalent of being cuddled and cared for by the mother? Transactional analysts coined the phrase stimulus-hunger a la food hunger as the prime mover in the social space and a problem to be solved. The epicentre of our engagement with the world is to search and find substitutes for the mothers' strokes of care-giving. The hunger for recognition is but a variant of the stimulus-hunger of childhood. Our social interactions are mutually reinforcing projects on the axis of recognition hunger. Our greetings, manners and social rituals are all expressions of this common project. After the greetings are exchanged, we have another problem to be solved. What do we do with each other, given that we have time on our hands? Eric Berne, the father of TA and also the author of this brilliant book *What Do You Say After You Say Hello*, called this as 'structure hunger'. When humans evolved into more and more social animals, the need to satiate structure hunger became a critical preoccupation. The uncomfortable silence in a social setting needs to be filled with some structure.

We fill this uncomfortable silence with three kinds of programmes, according to Berne. It can be material programme, that is, we are engaged in building something, whether building sandcastles in the beach or writing this book. It can be a social programme, with its ritualistic and semi-ritualistic undertones, for example, we go for a party or a picnic or to a religious ritual or simply gossip on the bench in the park. Soon these programmes acquire individual idiosyncrasies. This is when the social programme becomes an individual programme. When the social programme becomes an individual programme, it is subject to specific interpersonal dynamics. It is subject to incidents. These incidents are determined by the patterns of ego state interactions between the individuals. Such patterned transactions are the 'games people play' (also a popular book by Eric Berne).

In a nutshell, food hunger is satiated by food, stimulus-hunger by strokes, emotional hunger by recognition and boredom by structuring of our time.

We transact in the individual programming mode when one of the little people inside us—parent, adult or child—sends a stimulus to one of the little people inside the other person—parent, adult or child. For example, we ask our friend:

Me: How do I go to the mall?

Friend: It is near the sector 18 metro station, the e-rickshaw is the most convenient mode of transport and will cost you ₹30.

The little person inside the other person responds to this stimulus. The above, for example, is an adult-to-adult transaction. It is uncomplicated. It is complementary. Such a transaction pattern can go on uninterrupted. Each response in turn could become the stimulus, eliciting a counter-response and so on.

To introduce another concept, complementary transactions can go on while its opposite crossed transactions must result in the end of communication.

Consider this:

Mother: Why did you miss your tiffin box at school?

Daughter: Sorry ma, I forgot, will be careful from now on.

The stimulus is from the parent ego state of the mother. It could be construed as either a nurturing parent or critical parent from the tone of her voice. The response of the daughter is from her adaptive child. Recall, the adaptive child wants to obey or conform to injunctions laid down by parents or parental figures. This is also a complementary transaction. It is a parent-to-child and child-to-parent transaction.

Consider the following transaction between two friends:

Friend 1: We need to exercise; else, we could become obese. How about a walk today evening?

Friend 2: Speak for yourself dear!

While Friend 1 initiated an adult-to-adult stimulus, Friend 2 initiated a child (little professor) to parent (critical parent) response. The transactions cross, bringing an end to the interaction. Had Friend 2 retorted with either 'Sure, evening works' or 'How about morning before breakfast?' it would have been a complementary transaction. It would have ended with a solution being found, not in a speechless hurt person as far as this thread of conversation is concerned. The little professor in Friend 2 inappropriately bubbled up to respond.

Consider the following transaction between two seniors at college:

Senior 1: Now that the fresh batch has come, it is our duty to tell them the dos and don'ts at our institution so that they don't get lost.

Senior 2: Indeed, we must provide them demonstrable guidelines of behaviour in different situations (with a wink) like we did last year and seniors do every year.

Senior 1: We should not delay such matters, let us begin tonight!

Senior 2: OK, I will brief our other batchmates!

The overt transaction here is adult-to-adult stimulus and an adult-to-adult response. This is what is happening at the social level. The covert transaction is happening between the child ego states of the seniors and implicitly they are planning to rag the juniors that night. This covert transaction is happening at the psychological level.

When there is a difference between the overt and covert view on the transaction, it is called duplex transaction. It is a finer manoeuvre in the conversation, one that structures time, makes it interesting, re-affirms one's positions and consummates in a game.

Could you reflect on your transaction patterns today? Take a casual transaction you initiated today with an individual you are not very familiar with. A transaction, in hindsight, you believe did not go well. Did you or the other person indulge in a crossed transaction? How could you have averted this? Which ego state initiated the stimulus? From which ego state of the other person did the response come from?

My own casual transaction recently went like this:

....

Me: Need a packet of corn.

Shopkeeper: Take this. (Hands over a large ₹70 packet, gets busy on his phone and simultaneously tries to bill it.)

Me: (Motioning him to hold; I am hurt that he is busy on his phone and *did not even 'recognize' me.* I dial home.) He has frozen corn and the price is ₹70.

Spouse: He is giving you a large one, we don't need it, come home, I will make the soup without corn.

Me: (Frustrated pause) Hmm.

Spouse: It is palak soup, can be made without corn also.

Me: (After disconnecting phone) Don't you have a smaller packet?

Shopkeeper: Here it is (for ₹35).

Me: (Triumphant that I have got the right quantity and price, anticipating a favourable reaction at home, but a little annoyed that the shopkeeper gave the bigger packet) Bhaiya, this is packed on September 2017; earlier, the large packet was packed on December 2017.

Shopkeeper: (Now annoyed) Sir, it has 12 months validity.

Me: But…. (Implying 'can you find me a latter packaged piece?')

Shopkeeper: This is what I have. (Putting the smaller packet back in its place in an irritated manner)

Me: Alright, give it … can I Paytm?

Shopkeeper: (Showing the place to Paytm) Of course, haven't you Paytm-ed here before?

Me: Oh…. There is no signal; let me pay you by cash only.

....

A TA of the above episode:

My initial stimulus was from the adult ego state. The shop-keeper's manner and 'take whatever I give' attitude came from the critical parent. Probably, it was the anchoring effect of the phone call he was making. This was an inappropriate response from him. The little professor in me wanted to teach him a lesson and simultaneously provoked a parental response in my spouse. My spouse's initial critical parent response mellowed later to an adult recovery. As a matter of fact, *palak* (spinach) soup is embellished with corn but this is not an essential ingredient. Now, on enquiry about a smaller packet, the shopkeeper's own little professor gets conned in its own game; he hands over sheepishly like an adaptive child. Now this provokes a further little professor response in me, so I point out the date of packaging. The shopkeeper, already in a parental mode, thanks to the other call, now switches to critical parent. I give in like an adaptive child. However, I have got the recognition he denied me in the first place.

I could have steered the transaction differently. I could have politely told him to finish his call. He could have come back to his adult ego state. He could also have belligerently continued in which case I would have the option of walking away. I could have told him that I need a smaller quantity or enquired how long does it lasts once the packet is opened.

TA is actually a good tool for story-telling and creative writing. It can illustrate the essence of the dialogue and drama very well. About 30 years ago, there was a popular ad that won many awards for conveying the essence of family conversation and promoting the 'Idhayam' brand of gingley oil.

The ad is in Tamil; I am giving the English translation:

Wife—from the adult ego state:

Dear, when you come back do get a pack of Idhayam gingley oil.

Husband—from the adult ego state:

What is so special?

Wife—from the child ego state:

One can make bajji, vada, puri and lots of things and it has no cholesterol.

Husband—from the child ego state:

Is it so?

Wife—from the parent ego state:

These are all the home makers' arena. Did I ask you to wash clothes, cook? If I ask you to get Idhayam oil, why don't you simply get it?!

I believe this ad became popular because it represented the patterned game that husbands and wives play in a middle-class social setting. This is also the target consumer for the brand.

Now, focus on transactions that you have with very familiar people. They could be your spouse at home, your boss or a co-worker. Try and recall a dialogue you had today morning verbatim. It is even better if you are able to jot it down.

My transaction today morning went something like this:

Spouse: I had asked you to make the payment and just pick up the grocery bag from downstairs. Can't you even take a 5-minute break?

Me: Oh OK, OK. (Went down and came back with the bag)

Me: Do you have ₹12 change, he does not have it and … OK, got it, returning back to give it. (Implying that it is not a 5-minute job)

Spouse: You should have asked the boy to accompany you and hand over the change from here itself!

(I settle down and bell rings again…, noise of my getting up)

Spouse: (Rushing) Hold, I am opening the door. (House-help walks in)

This one starts with my spouse as critical parent. I play the little professor trying to prove that you are not always right. She gets back confirming her own position that 'my husband is not good at these things'. At the next opportunity (the house-help knocking the door), I try the little professor trick again, but my spouse averts it quickly as the critical parent in her does not like to have fingers pointed at her. She always has to occupy the moral high ground!

Now this instance itself may be incidental but what is central is the pattern of interaction. She is playing to confirm the position that 'he is not good at these practical matters', while I am playing to confirm my position 'I told you so'.

People form positions (in common parlance stances) about the world by the time they are 7 or 8. It gives them a comfortable assumption about the world and which is in agreement with their typical experiences. They live their life seeking, as a rule, confirmation of their stances or positions. When two people with complementary positions meet, they can skilfully manoeuvre every transaction to confirm their respective positions. The alternative of 'having no position' burdens the adult with how to respond at each instance. By living out pre-settled positions, most of life can be led on auto-pilot. This is equivalent to our snappy faster selves that Daniel Kahneman alludes to.

If we lead our lives on such an auto-pilot, we are not living it but merely passing through it. If we lead our lives on auto-pilot, the dysfunctional patterns will repeat. We don't make any active choices and life becomes happenstance. Our lives don't tell a unique story. Like games, they become semiconscious transactions progressing towards a predetermined outcome. We cannot have well-being in such a life much as a wall can have well-being or an animal with very limited freedom of behaviours. Breaking this pattern has been the source of joy. Across cultures and epochs, this has been the holy grail of well-being.

How Do We Break Free?

Firstly, we need to diligently cultivate an awareness of this aspect of ourselves. Unless it is deep-rooted, just awareness itself will pave the way for correction: yes, often such self-diagnosis itself is therapeutic. Secondly, we must be vigilant in contexts where we tend to automatically resort to them and prevent them as far as we can without embarrassingly rupturing ongoing transactions. We must experiment alternative life positions, stances and alternative reactions which we could rehearse and routinize privately.

Understanding our life positions brings us insight on how we engage with the world. We can examine dysfunctionalities, remove positions that do not conform to current realities and lead more spontaneous lives. Games we play with others are a vivid illustration of the positions we hold in un-examined auto-pilot modes.

HAPPINESS MANTRA

Develop the habit of watching your transactions and also observing dysfunctional interactions at your office amongst your colleagues. Find the point of crossed transactions and mentally substitute with an alternative response. Examine the beliefs that will make this alternative and more useful response possible. Create a daily journal of such observations.

Games We Play

A game is a patterned transaction moving to a predetermined outcome. We play games with people with whom we have significant interactions. We have rituals and pastimes with casual acquaintances. This pattern of interaction with the other defines our relationship. We both—ourselves and our counterparts—play this game because we are able to reinforce our respective positions about life. This is the gain or advantage the players derive from playing games. This reinforcement makes the world more familiar. Sometimes, this familiar picture is not the true picture of the world. The more there is a dissonance between the familiar picture and the real picture, our engagement with the world becomes that much dysfunctional. The larger the distance, the more neurotic we are.

There are typical games we play. They confirm some typical positions. These positions introduce the distortions that many amongst us suffer from. Our scores to several items, when we self-diagnose ourselves, are rooted in these positions.

The below is a real dialogue between the head of a business and his direct reportee, also a senior leader (general manager [GM]) in a company. They are also talking separately to the business' HR partner.

....

HR: Hi, good to see you after sometime. When did you come? You wanted to meet?

GM: Yes, landed last evening, did you have a word with Sujoy?

HR: He told me you had concerns and that after I speak to you he would discuss further. Other than this, I do not have any other background.

GM: It is about my empowerment and recognition. I am not able to grow because of perceptions people have. I would have quit long time ago, but for Sujoy. He has been supportive and requested me to overlook these irritants and focus on the job.

HR: David, I want to be honest with you. I did table your concerns recently about growth. After consideration, the answer was negative. The company values your contribution and I genuinely believe you are paid well but are not OK to promote you at this moment. You are already aware of the standards we apply for progression to the next level.

GM: I took up all difficult jobs only because of Sujoy. I hope you appreciate that to pull us out of that rut with that client took some doing.

HR: If you believe so, do you want to ask Sujoy to hand over the entire client unit to you?

GM: Ah, I don't know his considerations. I have no objections.

HR: Let me speak to him about it. Will you be willing to go to a unit which will provide progression and a different role?

GM: (Nervously) What will it entail? You know work content and boss are very important to me. I am getting both in good measure here.

⁛ ⁛ ⁛

HR: Got a minute. I finished a long discussion with David.

Head: I am aware, he did brief me.

HR: Why don't you hand over the entire unit to him? We can make a good case for progression.

Head: He will not be able to handle it.

HR: Does he agree too?

Head: I have been using him for his strengths. Unfortunately, he can't do this alone.

HR: It will be good to give him this feedback. Shall we do a 3-way meeting/call?

Head: I will take care of it Sravan. Let me know what best we can do to recognize the guy.

HR: You know it as much as I do Sujoy. In this year, we can't do much.

Head: I know. We must think of something....

⁛ ⁛ ⁛

Head: David, I spoke to HR and we will try to do something.

GM: Will I get promoted?

Head: Unlikely. There is some interesting opportunity coming up in the business which we must focus on David.

GM: Sure thing. What is it about? Just want you to take care of my recognition. I trust you to do the right thing.

Head: We will do our best.

HR: Did you guys speak?

GM: Yes, we did. He asked me to focus on business you know. That comes first. I have aired my concerns and he said he will consult you and do the best.

HR: I see.

GM: Even 9 months ago, the issue I raised is not resolved. Had he pushed it harder, I might have got the recognition.

HR: Did you think of the rotation to a new unit?

GM: Frankly, I have not devoted much time to it.

HR: Hmmm…. Do let me know if I have to explore.

Psychologists would call the game played here, 'If it weren't for you'/'If it weren't for him'. The aim of this game is re-assurance. The GM is speaking from his child ego state—a grouchy one. The head is coming from an adult ego state and sometimes that of a parent. The moment the head stops playing parent and dares the GM to make his choice, the GM gets very upset. He entices the head back into the game by putting the ball back in his court. The head falls for this bait and affirms his position that he knows what is best for everyone, and re-affirms his position 'but for me, you would be in a worse off position'. When he does fall for the bait, the psychological transaction becomes child-to-child, even as the social transaction is parent-to-child. The head is indulging in 'You will mess yourself up'. The GM in this game affirms his position that 'but for the head, he would have progressed well'. It is not the reality, but it is the reality that he wants to believe in. Whenever there is a possibility of this assumption getting shattered, the GM becomes nervous. His psychological transaction subtly gets into 'protect me'. In between, the manipulative little professor in the GM sees if there can be a good deal to be stuck here. The HR partner subtly stays clear of such a deal by focusing on the adult.

If we analyse the transaction between the HR partner on the one hand and each of the head and the GM on the other, another game is being played here. The HR partner desperately wants to 'cure' this misconception of the GM and the head, something he believes he can do and is well qualified to do. He plays the therapist assuming that the other parties want to get cured. He proposes an alternative without appreciating the subtler life positions of the head and the GM. The HR partner says, 'Why don't you... (align the entire unit)' to which the head replies, 'Yes, but... (he will mess it up)'. Similarly, he turns to the GM and says, 'Why don't you... (seek a transfer if you believe that it is because of him your career is stalled', to which the GM responds too quickly, 'Yes, but... (boss and work content are very important to me).' The GM is only seeking re-assurance and not a solution. It is the HR partner's lack of insight and his own position of 'I can solve his problem' that is prompting him to indulge in this game.

Games like these are played all the time. They have multiple advantages to the players. Firstly, the game contributes to their internal psychological stability, the position they want to re-affirm to themselves in all their transactions. It contributes to external psychological stability by studiously avoiding anxiety-arousing situations and intimacy. It also, after all, helps all parties get rid of their structure hunger!

The following four games are played often in work settings. This is in addition to 'If it weren't for you' as well as 'Why don't you, yes but' we saw illustrated in the above dialogues.

1. I told you so...

We encounter some characters in office and in our life whose position is 'I am always right'. They would typically offer some vague advice which is not specific or actionable. When the dreaded event does happen, they will chime in with an 'I told you so'. If the dreaded event does not happen, they will quietly slip away. There is anyway little danger of them getting pulled up when negative events do not happen. They often play with the victim who wants to play the next game—'why it always happens to me.'

2. **Why does it always happen to me?**

The primary aim of this game is for the person to re-affirm the life position that they are 'not OK'. In TA terms these are people who have grown up feeling inadequate about themselves. They believe that they will mess up things or unfortunate things will happen to them. In casual conversations they would portray themselves as the centre of tragedy. They love the attention of being the most impacted. They want to prove themselves that their misfortunes are greater than anyone else's.

3. **See what you made me do**

Here the game player transfers the guilt and the agency of a misfortune onto another person who just came to the scene. They would almost seduce someone to interrupt them and at that instance will mess things up and then transfer the onus on to the visitor with a 'see what you made me do'. Bosses may ask for teams' opinion and collect multiple opinions. If the misfortune occurs, they will then blame it on one of the opinions that they would claim they followed.

4. **Now I've got you, you son of a bitch (NIGYSOB)**

The game player tempts the other person to make an erroneous move. They may create the necessary preamble by stating that 'I hope ... such and such a thing won't happen' which will be a vague statement. Due to any uncertainty if even a part of this vague statement comes true, they will cry foul. They want to re-affirm their position that they are 'OK' and others are certainly 'not OK.'

Have you been able to catch yourself playing games recently? What kind of positions you were trying to affirm to yourself? Could you try and step aside from this position and consider alternative possibilities? Rigid labels and positions are a distortion of the world according to the cognitive behaviour therapists. TA helps you identify the games you play and the unexamined positions you assume.

By analysing your transactions, you will uncover the veil of a personal distortion, see the world for what it is and progress to greater well-being.

HAPPINESS MANTRA

If you or another person whom you do business with play either—'See what you made me do' or 'I told you so' or 'NIGYSOB' or 'Why does it always happen to me' or 'If it weren't for you' or 'Why don't you, yes but', pause. See the futility of game playing and the rigidity of positions that is preventing you from growing. Create a daily journal of games you or others played and explore the origin of the positions.

A Journal of Mistakes, Forgetfulness and Errors

Through his book *The Psychopathology of Everyday Life*, Sigmund Freud opened our eyes to the power of the unconscious, our own unconscious. By investigating a very innocuous phenomenon—the slips of everyday life, he threw light on mental processes 'which' intend something else. By accepting the existence of such mental processes and acknowledging their intentions, he intended to cure the psyche of its pathology. These pathological states are the stuff of everyday life in normal people.

In our journey to well-being, we may wisely access this second tool to spot, acknowledge and handle the pathologies of our own everyday life. While using TA as a tool for well-being, we reflected back on our transactions and transaction patterns. We then derived insights on the crossed transactions we make and our own dysfunctional patterns of transactions. Through these crossed transactions and games we play, we tried to examine our own positions. By creating a safe space to examine and reduce the impact of our positions, we tried to live well.

In the analysis of errors, we will likewise explore 'when' we make those errors and 'what' they may mean. It is hard to recall an error. It may be easier to catch yourself committing an error. Have you wondered why we slip up, make an error? In honour of Freud, these slips are called the Freudian slips.

Freud first considered and refuted explanations for our slip-ups and inadvertencies as occurring due to fatigue. He cleverly pointed out that if fatigue or a physiological disturbance were the cause, the substitution or distortion can be vast and varied. He had repeatedly observed that even the distorted expression or act was a meaningful one. It is however, an unpalatable meaning. We want to suppress this meaning to ourselves and others.

Despite the watchful gaze of the superego (our moral self) and the ego (our realistic self and persona), the id (our instinctual self) manages to transmit the message through the slip-up. This fleeting glance at our unconscious processes can provide useful clues on things that we dare not admit even to ourselves. Uncovering and acknowledging these urges is a critical component of peak mental health. There are several types of slip-ups.

In speech, we sometimes catch ourselves saying the exact opposite of what we had wished. Sometimes the wrong expression is a mixture of two competing expressions. We discover that we have suddenly gone blank when we are trying to help someone or give them a tip. Often, we are unable to recall proper names. When we do try and recall this name through another name, even this one slips out. It is at the tip of our tongue but is lost. We also find that we are able to recall it a few moments later after the occasion had just passed. This forgetting of proper names is a very temporary forgetfulness. We mispronounce proper names or we substitute one proper name with another. This other name has a meaning for us. We mishear, misread and mistype. Often the misread or misheard word has a special meaning to us. We also mislay things, miss appointments. Mislaying things and missing appointments can happen repeatedly even after we have vowed to be careful to ourselves.

At its core, mistakes are psychic acts that occur when two conflicting intentions are trying to express themselves. Surely, some mistakes are physiological disturbances, but most are psychic acts. Especially, in the errors of the tongue slip type, the self is often unable to hear it. It needs a bit of practice to catch one committing an error. It is relatively easier to notice the errors that others' make. What exactly do these errors mean?

Forgetting Proper Names

Krishiv was scheduled to meet his interviewer for a potential job change. He wanted to 'google' the person the night before but postponed it to the next morning. He had to take an early morning flight the following day. He told himself that he would check out the profile on the way to the airport. Once on the taxi and after checking Google Maps that he is scheduled to reach on time, he set out to do the thing he had identified.

But…. (Blank)… What is the name of my interviewer? How would I search without the name? Why is such a familiar name now not accessible?

He had to actually search his emails and messages from the Headhunter to identify the name. He did the search and got prepared for the interview. Once at the company's office, once again his mind went blank when asked with whom he had an appointment. Last time he went blank, he had vowed not to forget this name by linking it with another famous person. Now, even this linked name was inaccessible. Embarrassed, he stood when fortuitously someone else mentioned this name at the reception and he was able to navigate through.

Analysis revealed that his agreeing to the interview was a half-hearted act. While the position was senior, the company was a smaller one. He was also not sure of its future prospects. He was also not sure if the new manager (the interviewer) will be inspiring.

One way to analyse is to free associate at the very point of becoming blank. Give yourself the mental permission to record any associations that come to your mind. To Krishiv, the following came to his mind:

Name—Limited; also—ran, second, stop-short, forgettable, boring, escapism, blind.

Based on this analysis, he has told himself that unless the deal is very good, he is going to refuse the offer. If he experiences any hesitation, he is going to set the default to 'don't take it'.

HAPPINESS MANTRA

If you catch yourself forgetting something and this surprises you, pause, tell yourself that it is OK to forget and suffer the consequences. One part of you is not convinced that what you are about to do is correct. If it is a name, you may also be having ambivalent feelings about this person, that is, you have a dislike that you don't wish to admit considering that it is not appropriate.

Following is an instance of competing expressions:

···

Competing Expressions

A not so easy restructuring was going on in a function when one of the persons facilitating had an unenviable task of managing conflicts in resource allocation to the new structure. She was dreading it. Here is an email she wrote to a select group. This is about the resources she recommends be pulled out from their existing teams and staffed in the newly constituted team in the restructured function.

> Hello All, Restricting this mail to ourselves as of now...
> PFB the names which have been identified for the track lead position
>
> 1. I have picked up the top 3 ratings for the last two years
> 2. Currently their role is to support at level 3 of organization or level 2
> 3. Few of them are quite long timers and understand the <u>nuisances</u> of the system as well.

···

She of course meant 'nuances' in her third point. Analysis revealed that she considered the whole assignment and especially this part of it such a nuisance. As she was readying herself for the long battle ahead and communicating her decision, the conflicting thought substituted the word 'nuisance' for 'nuance'. She was also not sure if the said plan will work or if it will create more nuisances.

HAPPINESS MANTRA

A slip of the tongue or a compounding of two words is just an interference of conflicting thoughts. It merits understanding this conflict and if possible resolving it. At the least, admit this conflict exists clearly and squarely to yourself.

Forgetting Resolutions and Impressions

This is the third time Vijay forgot to enquire about the passport. The family had planned a trip to Thailand. In the last trip within India, there was such a misunderstanding between him and his spouse on what places to visit. While coming back, they wondered why they went out for this trip. He had gotten over it, he told himself, and it is 2 years since they all went anywhere. He genuinely resolved to figure out if the police verification is successful and the passport will be obtained. He had heard from his accounts head to not indulge in rules arguments to the visiting cop. He registered it or so he thought.

At the first instance, he argued with the cop. The family was away for two days then. This put the passport verification process into a spin. Now that this was sorted out with four times the effort, the mere enquiry of if everything is in order was getting forgotten.

His friend had given a contact who had the access to confirm if all is in order. It was far easier than standing in the long queues. Nevertheless, this is the third day he is forgetting to speak to this contact.

First he dialled a wrong number, and then he stored this correctly on his smartphone. Next, he forgot the application number. This third attempt, he simply missed calling the gentleman at 11 AM, the time he had given to call.

The analysis here is obvious. A painful memory of the last vacation has not been gotten over with, unlike what the conscious self believed. His subconscious is actually plotting for Vijay to forget the third time.

HAPPINESS MANTRA

The origins of our forgetfulness or mislaying of objects is usually an unpleasant association the object forgotten has with an imminent event or recent event. Admit your feelings to yourself. Make a conscious compromise in case you wish to or have to move ahead in the original direction. This way the journey and the execution will be less stressful.

Erroneously Carried out Actions

I had once gone to another centre of ours in a different city. I usually stay there for a subsequent day after our regular meetings. Since the trip went as per plan, I was in a good mood. I had met my extended team as well as a few managers from the business. Our conversations became informal. There were some in-progress discussions with the corporate office which were confidential in nature. In my enthusiasm, I had revealed quite a bit of it to one of the teams and to my extended team. They seemed to be lapping every bit of this advance information. I suddenly realized I had opened up too much. Subsequently, I tried to disclaim whatever I said with some counter-perspectives. I took the initiative to erase what I had written on the whiteboard with a marker. As the line managers left, one of my direct reports also alluded to the fact that I gave much information out. I denied it stating that I was only speculating. When it was time to go to the airport, I quickly packed my stuff and rushed.

When I came to my home location, I discovered that I had also picked up the whiteboard eraser (duster) and it is in my bag. I was worried if it was instead of the laptop charger, in which case I will be severely handicapped. To my surprise, the laptop charger was there as well. I was then comparing the sizes and weights of both. It would take a stretch to pick up one, thinking it is the other.

The analysis on this was straightforward. I had extended myself in revealing stuff. I had to somehow erase this. I had done a second uncomfortable act by saying that I did not reveal too much. I had to take the weapon (whiteboard eraser) from the scene of the crime for me to feel comfortable.

HAPPINESS MANTRA

Create a journal of errors, mistakes and forgetting. After you have reached 30 entries, study what it reveals about you, the conflicts you undergo and the choices you could exercise. Write down some potential choices for your consideration. Sleep over these choices and if it is easy, implement them.

Mislaying Things

I had a functional meeting to attend on the 7th, 8th and 9th. I also had a business meeting to attend on the 6th and 7th. I feel that these long two or three-day meetings are unproductive. Folks put their teams under pressure so that they look the best amidst the peer group and the boss. This results in no real problems getting discussed and the teams also lose their productivity trying to prepare for this jamboree. It is of course politically incorrect to express such things. I have often boasted to my colleagues that I don't waste the time of the team asking them to prepare a presentation for me so I look good in front of my boss or peers. This particular meeting was important for this is the first one with our new boss. He could be forming some lasting impressions. But I was steadfast on my ideals to not trouble the team too much. In fact, when they asked if I needed any support and I said 'No', I felt good.

Similarly, I also had to prepare for a business meeting on the 7th, which I advanced to 6th because of this conflict. Instead of the usual—'what are you happy or unhappy about?' kind of session we do in HR, I decided to change track and convert it into a learning session on 'how we make decisions?'

I wear two spectacles, one for reading and one for walking about. As I started the presentation to this group, I put my reading spectacles in the case in the podium and specifically told myself not to miss taking this back.

That said, I was wondering even if I should spend time to prepare for this functional meeting on the 7th. We can pick up slides from recent presentations and weave some sort of a story, I told myself. As I wound up the first presentation with business and chit-chatted, I had forgotten my reading glasses and went home.

One of the team members who was in both meetings brought it the next morning. Meanwhile, I assuaged myself that since I did not have the reading glasses, I can only do a last-minute slide preparation for the meeting with my new boss.

This is a classic tussle between the ego, the superego and the id. The superego asserted that burdening team for your presentation is no good. The ego felt a bit uncomfortable as it is not practical. There is an impression to manage. The id fundamentally rebelled against the idea of such wasteful meetings themselves. It somehow wanted a way out where it won't be burdened by the superego to prepare thoroughly. By cleverly missing to take the reading glasses despite an explicit reminder from the ego (the practical self), it got an escape route to relax without feeling too guilty.

HAPPINESS MANTRA

The proof of the removal of personal distortions is a light feeling of self-acceptance and feeling at ease. You will also be free from the need to pretend.

7

Well-being Through Dream Analysis

Why We Sleep?

In the violent world that our ancestors lived in, shut eye and paralyzed body are actually disadvantages for survival. What benefits occur in sleep that compensate for this risk of loss of life? Why do we sleep?

Studying sleep-deprived individuals versus normal individuals has given us clues to the benefits of sleep. Sleep deprivation results in an inability to form new memories. Sleep deprivation diminishes the functioning of the hippocampus in the brain. Hippocampus is associated with learning and memory. If we do not switch off and sleep after 16 hours of wakefulness, many of our abilities and health markers begin to deteriorate. We are unable to regulate our emotions. We get irrational and irritable, and can quickly switch to funny and quirky behaviour. We lose our emotional integrity and become vulnerable to wild mood swings. We quickly flit from one emotion to another, much like drunk people. Further, sleep deprivation produces symptoms very similar to psychotic disorders. Even a consistent, 25% sleep deprivation ages several physiological markers, like virility by a full 10 years. A 50% sleep deprivation for one night leads to a 75% reduction in performance of our immune system. Constant sleep deprivation to this tune, it is being suspected, makes us prone to even numerous forms of cancer. This has prompted the World Health Organization to declare sleep deprivation as a carcinogen.

During the deep sleep stage, the metabolic waste of the brain gets flushed. We become like 'dry sponges' ready to process new information and consolidate our memories, says Dr Mathew Walker. Sleep is the very foundation of well-being, not just one of its pillars, says Dr Walker.

There are five stages of sleep in a cycle of sleep each lasting 90–110 minutes. Each night, we go through 4 –6 such cycles. Stage 1 is winding down: When you drift off into sleep and momentarily wake up only to drift off again. Involuntary movement or jerking of muscles happens in stage 1. Stage 2 is where we spend the maximum amount of time, almost half the sleep cycle. The muscles relax, the heart rate slows down and the blood pressure falls in stage 2. The core body temperature also decreases in stage 2. This is a stage of light sleep. There is no eye movement in stage 2, and the brain waves also slow down. Stages 3 and 4 are the deeper sleep phases. There is no eye movement in stages 3 and 4 and the brain waves slow down to a greater extent. These waves are called delta waves. Stages 3 and 4 are also called slow wave sleep. Blood pressure drops even further and breathing gets slow, deep and rhythmic. Stages 3 and 4 are highly restorative for the body. Growth hormones are released in these stages. They repair the cells that got exerted during the day. The blood flow to the muscles increases providing oxygen and the much-needed nutrients. This is followed by stage 5. It is marked by rapid eye movements (REMs). The brain bursts with activity during this stage and almost resembles waking. Stage 5 lasts 20% of the duration of a typical adult sleep cycle. The eyes dart from here to there under the closed eyelids while the muscles remain paralyzed. Breathing becomes shallow and irregular and the blood pressure begins to rise. It is in stage 5 that we dream. The paralysis of our limbs and muscles ensures that we don't act out our dreams.

It has now been scientifically established that we all dream at least three dreams every night.

Why We Dream?

A final verdict on this question is yet to be pronounced. Initially, scientists believed that dreams are disturbed sleep. If we follow this hypothesis, we need to explain then what causes dreams. Again the initial belief was that dreams are caused by somatic interference. Somatic interference is literally interference from or on the body. External sensory information such as light, sound or touch disturbs our sleep and our mind conjures up images and stories. Even internal bodily stimuli such as palpitations, full bladder or a blocked nose are loosely represented in dream content. Personally, we can attest to this fact. We have had dreams when external stimuli has been transformed and presented in a dream to us. Maury, in a self-experiment, arranged to smell cologne while in the REM state. Freud illustrates this well in his lectures on psychoanalysis. As soon as he smelt cologne,

> Maury dreamed that he was in Cairo in the shop of Johann Marina Farina, and therewith were linked some extravagant adventures. Or, when a drop of water was poured on his forehead, he dreamt then that he was in Italy, perspiring profusely, and drank the white wine of Orvieto.

The connection between the somatic stimulus and the dream is obvious. But what caused the extravagant adventures and what about the white wine? Why should we invent a full story of which the somatic stimuli are mere trigger? Is there any more meaning to these full stories? Are these merely electro-chemical disturbances?

The full stories are memory associations. They are not true to life because the ego that keeps our thinking within the contours of reality is off duty when we sleep. We are all in a way neurotic and dissociated from reality when we dream. They can be improper because the superego or the moral principle is also inactive in our dream state. We loosen up when we dream. We are imaginative when we dream. It is an effortless kind of imaginativeness. The next logical question is why this particular dream? Why should this story be presented out of many possible stories even if a dream is triggered by somatic disturbances?

Freud found clues to answer these questions from the everyday language about dreams. We use the word 'day dreams'. What do we really mean? Is it our infantile self trying to picture its wish getting fulfilled? Is it a remnant from the days of infancy when the boundaries of the self with the world are not yet firmed up? Is it a carryover from the phase of life when we fondly thought our writ runs on the world, only to be reminded that we need to cry even to get suckled? Yes, dreams *are* expressions of wish fulfilments.

Freud analysed his and others' dreams and found some more common characteristics. Each dream had a manifest content and a latent content. The objects, settings, the characters, the plot and the outcome are just not exactly the impersonal objects, settings, characters, plot and outcomes that we experience in the wake state. They have personal and deeper meanings for the dreamer. Freud uncovered these personal meanings by a technique called 'free association'. Either the dreamers themselves or the initial promptings of the analyst convinced them that the dream had a hidden message. Yes, every dream has *a hidden message—from you, to yourself!*

Dreams seem to be triggered by some event of the previous day. Freud found that it is not the event itself but our half-hearted and muted reaction to it that precipitates the dream. It is called 'Day Residue'. It settles down deep in our mind and bubble up during the dreaming phase of our sleep cycle. Ayurveda rightly characterized dreams 'as symptoms of mental indigestion'. It is similar to the beliefs about ghosts: Well-lived and well buried people don't become ghosts. Folks who were not at peace with their lives and to whom the living did not grant a decent send-off did become ghosts. It is the same with thoughts and feelings it seems. These are thoughts and feelings of the previous day. Yes, every dream is precipitated by an undigested *residue* of the previous day.

Psychologists uncovered two more truths about dreams. The latent content of dreams alluded to a present moment dilemma confronting the dreamer. The content of any dream also has a chain of associations to events of the past beyond the previous day. Of course, they have to be from the dreamers' own past. What was intriguing was that many dreams seem to be also pointing to wishes, hurts and other overwhelming experiences of *childhood*. Hidden or latent thoughts about a dilemma as well as experiences from early life are present in each and every dream.

And why must any dream content be hidden? Dreams are after all arbitrary, at least on the face of it. The ego and super-ego, while less dominant in the dream state, are not wholly suppressed. Just like in the waking state the ego and superego puts a lid on the activities of the id, they do so in the dream state too but far less effectively. Even while we dream, our moral selves censor. The id, therefore, disguises the wishes it is struggling to express in symbolic language. At the same time, the function of dreams is to release the pressure built up during the day, much like a safety valve. This pressure release gives us a chance to re-engage with the world the very next day without the burden of unattended baggage. Releasing pressures as well as couching and censoring them are the twin forces every dream navigates every night.

Every dream is thus also a distorted neurotic expression of a forbidden thought and emotion. Every dream is a vehicle for expressing hidden wishes. Every dream is a safety valve that heals our wounds and releases our stresses. Every dream is another shot at the dilemmas of the day. Every dream, in Freud's words, is 'a royal road to the unconscious'. We can certainly call the interpretation of our dreams as a royal road to our well-being.

How exactly to take this high road to well-being?

Retrieving and Recording Your Dreams

It has been proved by sleep laboratory experiments that we have at least three dreams every night. However, most of us forget our dreams. It is critical to record one's dreams as soon as one wakes up. Yes, on most of the days we wake up from a dream. It is natural as it is the last stage of the sleep cycle—the REM stage. We wake up typically realizing how external stimuli—a pillow touching our hand or an alarm—have become part of the dream content. To recall a dream well, we must refocus on what we dreamt as soon as we wake up. We must do this without moving our bodies. Studies have further found that shaking yourself when you get up can make you forget your dream. It is also useful to recall the very last scene of the dream—the last 5–10 seconds at the point of waking up. Catching the tail of the dream is natural and easier. Then you can follow the thread of the dream memory backwards as far as you can go. When it gets harder, retrace the path of the thread forward. Don't try to edit away the inconsistencies. It is not a dry cognitive recollection. Try to 're-live' the dream. This backward–forward exercise on the 'royal road to the unconscious' will consolidate the narrative content of the dream alive.

Most of our dreams are visual. This is so despite non-visual external stimuli and internal somatic stimuli impinging on our dreaming psyche. A very small part of our dream content, if at all, is auditory, although, of all the five sensory stimuli, auditory stimuli have the highest chance of impinging on our dreams. Predominantly, dreams are non-verbal phenomena unless the very theme of the dream is about words. The scripts we attribute to the characters in our dreams are a later superimposition. It is we who put words into the mouth of the characters when we narrate a dream after we wake up. Dreams are like the silent films of the last century.

Again, our wake state language is not adequate to express exhaustively the contents of our dreams. The recordings of dreams suffer from this translation of a visual dream into a verbal narrative. Carolyn Winget and Milton Kramer in their book *Dimensions of Dreams* undertook the most extensive consolidation of attempts to objectify dreams. As a by-product, they gave us a systematic questionnaire that aided dream recall. It consists of eight cues about the generic content elements of dreams. They are: emotions, setting[s], objects, characters, activities, interactions, outcome[s] and overall environment. These eight elements can serve you well to recall your dream accurately.

What is the 'setting'? In which place and time do the dream scenes occur? Sometimes the dream setting changes as the dream moves on and each setting is reckoned as a scene. More specifically, the time of the year, for example, season, and the time of the day, for example, morning, evening and night, also comprise the setting.

Which are the 'objects'? For example, is it sofa, clock, dining table, TV?

Who are the 'characters'? It could be the primary characters who are interacting or doing some activity in the scene and the secondary characters, which are present but do not participate in any activity or interaction.

What are the 'activities'? It could be opening a door, driving or even sleeping carried out by individuals in the dream episode.

What are the 'interactions'? It is something done by two or more characters in the dream episode. It could be fighting, quarrelling, cooperating in a hunt or game of soccer, conversing, etc.

What is the 'outcome'? At the end of this episode what do the activities and interactions result in?

What are the 'emotions' that the primary characters are expressing or experiencing?

Whether the overall 'environment' is pleasant or unpleasant, happy or sad, favourable or unfavourable?

While recording the dream, an automatic orientation to these eight aspects ensures that copious material is dredged out and made available for interpretation. I recommend an individual and private dream diary in which to record your dreams with dates. This structure of dream recall also facilitates its interpretation.

HAPPINESS MANTRA

Develop the habit of recording dreams and at least get to the day's residue that precipitated the dream. A review of residues over time will tell you your points of resistance and the places where you blink/distort reality.

Carrying out Dream Analysis

After the dream has been written or spoken into a Dictaphone or your mobile phone, it can be interpreted. Distinguishing between the exact dream content and further collateral thoughts about it that pop during recall is an important part of the recording process. A popular technique to interpret the dream is 'free association'.

Free association starts with a 'stimulus word' and the subject is asked to produce all the things that come to his/her mind. No effort should be put in to think or logically reason the link between the stimulus word and the subsequent things recalled. The subject is encouraged to be uninhibited and report everything that comes to his/her mind. These associations are recorded. The inhibition-less and fantasy-like characteristic of the association makes it 'free' association. Freud makes a strong claim that the next word that you free-associate is in fact the only word you will free associate. It is a wholly determined affair. What determines the next word is not the cognitive thinking process but our inner psychological complexes. In other words, free association is and must be an undertaking that is triggered and powered by a psychological momentum in the individual; any logical nexus in the chain of words is incidental.

When free association is done with the elements of a dream, the stimulus acquires a new significance. Recall that the generic elements of a dream are: setting, objects, activities, interactions, characters, emotions, outcome(s) and environment. The elements are embedded in a web of associations without a centre. Somewhere in these associations, there is a knot which is a personal psychological complex. It is natural that the association exercise sheds more light on the complex. Just like the errors of waking life had in them unconscious impulses which were not directly accessible, so does the whole dream has a secret message. Free association reveals things we wanted to say but have instead substituted with other elements in our dream. This is because directly confronting them would have been unthinkable. An analysis of free associated outputs to the dream elements is a way of getting around to this secret message. Yes, the royal road to the unconscious is indeed devious!

HAPPINESS MANTRA

Try to analyse at least one dream every week. This will give you rich data of your unconscious and will help you truly know what your heart desires. It can give you useful clues for personal change or adjusting better with your environment.

Dreams Are Wish Fulfilments

Freud boldly asserted that every dream is an expression of the fulfilment of a wish. This is our selfish id at work. These wishes are stopped in their track by our censoring system whenever they run up against social norms. The id manages to sneak it (the wish) in a camouflaged form into the dream content. Even dreams that are apparently the reverse of a wish—unpleasant or painful ones—on interpretation were found to have a wish-fulfilling element in them. The proof of this will requires extensive analysis and examples. This will distract us from the application of dream interpretation for well-being. So I am skipping this line of thought. Interested readers can follow it up with leads in the bibliography section.

In children, dreams are undisguised wish fulfilments. For example:

A small boy of 5 dreamt that he was eating lots of perk chocolate, and he remembers to be biting them and fully hearing the sound of the bite.

In the previous evening a bar of perk was denied to him for fear of tooth decay by his mother. He was planning to have it anyway without his mother's concurrence.

In adults, the wishes maybe more disguised. Here, is a one of my recent dreams:

The setting seemed to be my IIT Madras lab where an Iyengar faculty (am unable to recollect his name now, but he wore a distinct tilak and also had a tuft of hair tied at the back like orthodox Brahmins do) was supervising. I could see five of us at different long tables typical of labs. My schoolmate Vijaya and my IITM class fellow Mathangi are at one of the tables. Rajesh, also an IITM classmate, known for his communist views, is discussing something with them. Another Rajesh (who is from the town of Madurai, brilliant but a bit reclusive) is by himself. I am doing my experiments on one of the tables. This joint activity, I surmise, will make us all closer friends. There is a light, the typical one glowing above us—actually a pair of tube lights in a single casing, slightly worn out with dark patches on the sides. It reminded me of the ear-piece section of my mobile phone in terms of its look. It also resembled a centipede—an insect with several legs. We hand the results over to this faculty and I suddenly see myself going through several dark rooms (like you see in the last scene of Jurassic Park, when the children get caught as they are having food, with dinosaurs sneaking in). Then, some more dark rooms. Later, I emerge out from the side of a toilet, which partially reminds me of Vivekananda College. There are rows of cycles parked close to each other—a typical sight. If one cycle falls, all of them fall—like a domino. Partially, the setting resembles that from my childhood days when I had attended an important relative's wedding. We had slept in the marriage hall, not the most convenient of places and I was woken up to take bath, think at 4:30 AM or 5 AM to hurry up and get ready when the bathrooms were free. In the dark, I found it both fearsome (that I could get lost) and inconvenient.

The above is, of course, the manifest dream content. This along with the latent dream thoughts could hold a clue to the interpretation of the dream. Several of the manifest elements could be traced to events of the previous day. Here, are a few and also notice how they were repressed because they were unpleasant.

I was teaching science to my son at home. I was struggling to explain the difference between insects and birds. We tried size, he conjectured that insects are dirty, birds are not! The only thing I could come up with was that insects had many legs and even on this feature I was not sure. I thought for a moment that my science bearings have worn out and dismissed this unpleasant thought even as it arose.

Yesterday, Vijaya, a schoolmate, sent me a link through WhatsApp about the controversy surrounding a film lyricist and his re-telling of the story of Andal, a revered saint in the Brahminical Iyengar pantheon. What was striking about the link was that the author of the link criticized this lyricist as misapplying archaic and non-modern work like that of Freud and Marx. The article also talked about bridal mysticism. Wasn't

I too applying Freud in this book I am writing? Isn't Freud controversial? What if it misfires? All these thoughts were not allowed to rise to the surface of consciousness at all. I appreciated how Vijaya sent the material in a balanced manner; other Iyengars would have been more emotional.

I was trying to help draw a mobile phone for my son's homework and noticed the ear-piece area is shaped like a centipede. The assignment was on 'modern' means of communication.

Before sleeping, I saw a WhatsApp from my Vivekananda College classmates about someone teasing a bull with a song and the bull charging and felling the individual who was singing and dancing before it. I had shown it to my son.

The dream has much material for an elaborate interpretation. We will content ourselves with uncovering some hidden strands in the dream thoughts. We have to stop as deeper uncovering will be detrimental to my sense of privacy.

The latent dream thoughts had to do with anxiety about relying on Freud for this chapter of my work. This is also about the fear that it may backfire. The fact that multiple types of individuals were doing the experiment with me including a communist friend, an indifferent person, two Iyengars who could get offended, is my psyche trying to play up the possibilities. That the lab-in-charge was an Iyengar too and his comforting demeanour is a prognosis for a normal outcome for the book. The tube light above looking like a centipede and like the ear-piece of my mobile phone—a modern means of communication—is again comforting. That there are two tube lights and how redundancy is provided for, one will function even if the other goes off, indicates a way out of the dilemma. Subsequently, free association of the rows of cycles equated a cycle to be a chapter and a project. The book needs to diversify in its foundations is what I took away.

When I free associated with the number 2 (two lights for redundancy), the numbers 4 and 7 and its multiples suggested itself. On later retrospection, the idea of connecting chapters

2, 4 and this chapter turns out to be a good idea. It was a nice creative insight from my unconscious mind.

The dark rooms looking like Jurassic Park is the criticism of relying on archaic research—the dinosaur being an archaic animal. The transfer of anxiety in the children, who are being threatened to be gobbled up by this archaic dinosaur, is another indication to me to diversify the foundations of the work, separate the chapter into clear layers, so they all don't collapse like the row of cycles. Free association of centipede yielded *keeda*, also the colloquial Hindi word that represents the strong urge to do something.

The telescoping of childhood memories needs further exploration. The anxiety about being lost in bathing in the dark may be symbolic of trying to navigate the work or could signal something deeper. The bridal mysticism in the day's residue brought the marriage hall into the dream.

HAPPINESS MANTRA

Pay attention to the infantile material thrown up and childhood memories that dream interpretation alludes to. Ask yourself if these determined your personality and whether you wish to question this basis of your personality.

While interpreting dreams for others or for ourselves, we may confront an objection to probe further. We may experience 'resistance' and want to continue no further. They are usually instructive spots and in fact may hide more valuable insights.

You would also notice that the manifest content of the dream is small whereas the connected underlying latent dream thoughts are copious. In fact, the above dream interpretation has hardly been exhausted. Each element of the dream, including the tilak, the fact that I forgot the faculty's name (incidentally, it is Mr Sarangapani) are all significant. The tube light such as the one I described is what I used to stare up when the class was uninteresting or I was unable to follow. 'Tube light' in colloquial is one who is slow to understand.

Can you now see the association of trying to cope up and feeling inadequate? Is it not linked to repressed thoughts of the prior day? That I was unable to lucidly explain the differences between birds and insects to my son, recalled a similar predicament at my classes at IIT Madras when I used to stare at the tube light. Now the tube light, actually two of them, with black edge, symptoms of ageing, got fused to the image of the insect. The unconscious chose this image as it is a fusion of both the predicaments (not being able to explain to my son and not being able to follow a lecture as a student) and is hence a richer symbol of meaning. The choice of elements is not arbitrary.

A dream has several layers of meaning indeed! One superficial interpretation hardly does justice to the teeming depth that is our unconscious!

Did you notice that I have forgotten the name of the relative whose marriage I attended and felt lost? If this is probed well, it can yield many more insights. The phenomena of hiding copious material behind a few images and actions are the characteristic of all dreams. Freud gave the name 'condensation' to such a process. It is the equivalent of compressing (zipping) files that we undertake in our computers.

Another characteristic of dreams is displacement. Here, one person or one thing is substituted by another to effectively disguise the message. This is resorted to in order to slip through the censorship of the superego. The same event happening to a substitute dream character is more acceptable to the superego.

The dream that follows is an illustration of such a displacement. What sort of messages do our dreams convey? Spending time in interpreting dreams is directly pursuing well-being. How else would we have reached so many toxic unconscious thoughts detrimental to our well-being? How else would we have got clues to the resolution of our dilemmas? Without this process, we would have hardly understood that such a dilemma even exists. We live under the spell of several such nameless anxieties. Dreams tell us about our hidden wishes. Dream interpretation helps us become self-aware. They help us readjust and fine-tune ourselves to our own inner and outer worlds. They remove personal distortions in our perception of the world. Especially, they remove extreme fixations our waking self succumbs to. These extreme views are our neurotic superimposition on a less harmful reality.

Dreams hence clarify. They can unleash personal creativity. They can facilitate a personal change far more effectively and quickly than all the reasoning we do with ourselves. Some dream interpreters have been able to perceive brewing ailments. Dream interpretation allows us to 'effortlessly' self-introspect.

HAPPINESS MANTRA

When you are in a dilemma, you can literally sleep over it, perform dream analysis and gain useful perspectives on the decision alternatives. You would certainly know in which direction your well-being and happiness lies amongst the decision alternatives.

The dream below illustrates at once displacement, condensation, a present dilemma and infantile material. In this one, I am also giving the steps taken to interpret the dream. You could try to interpret your dreams just the way I have done here. The proof of correct interpretation is when you internally feel this is the truth or feel a sense of lightness or unburdening or as if something has been unknotted inside you. Ann

Faraday describes the discovery of the meaning of a dream as an 'aha' experience. She also says when we correctly discover the meaning of a dream 'it resonates in our bones'.

I dreamt this last weekend:

CVK (my present CEO) checked in to our house reporting that he is unbearably tired and his eyelids are forcing shut. As we opened the house, it looked like 32 VC Garden 2nd Street, at Chennai, my earlier residence, but when he finally rested at our bedroom on a mattress on the floor adjacent to the cot, it looked like Ram Vihar (my present residence). The house is unusually occupied with my sisters' children as well, my wife, mother and father. It appears my sisters are also there. The book shelf is visible. The mattress and the cover distinctly resemble the one that my father and eldest sister had for them at VC Garden street. It was light blue with dark blue lines in the shape of an 'L' drawn on it. What is striking is the way CVK is resting, on one hand, half lying and half sitting, very casually at this humble previous home of mine. His posture resembles that of Lord Ganesha at one end and the Facebook photograph of my former driver. CVK has a black pant and white half-sleeved shirt on him and seems to be relishing his rest. The bed has a bit of water and I am a bit embarrassed, but he seems to be ok with it and lies down on the dry portions. My mother then sits next to him and is cutting vegetables on the *aruvamanai* (a sickle-like object fastened to a wooden base) and casually asking what the matter with his health is and why he is not taking rest. I also indicate to her to give him space to rest. I feel an embarrassment at her direct approach, but CVK is at home. My father points to the cot and I request CVK to lie on the cot so he is not disturbed, give him blankets, switch on the fan, etc. Prior to this, we get talking about SG who also seems to be there timid, quite unlike him. I ask CVK, how he managed such collaboration between him and others. He says that they all went to the theatre (seemed like a Rajni or/and Kamal movie) and he fed SG 'molaga (chilly) bajji' which was very spicy. When he struggled for water to drink, he realized he had to depend on his team mates, who gave this to him. He is still reflecting on and recovering from this experience. I note down the easy cure CVK adopted and also its directness. I feel a bit sorry for SG but also like the lesson he learnt and the direct method CVK adopted. I woke up from the dream when CVK had comfortably settled on the cot and was about to fall asleep. By this time, I was out of the bed in the dream.

To de-construct the dream into its elements:

Setting[s]: Door and immediate space beyond it in 32 VC Garden 2nd Street and rest of house is F 124 Ram Vihar, in-between a theatre I have visited and probably sat in one of the earlier (front?) rows of seats (3–5). It is morning time; yet, it is a composite setting one dovetailing through a second one onto another.

Objects: Bed with the mattress on it which was used in that old house, the current cot and mattress, the old blanket that I had and subsequently my sister had, the book shelf in the corridor, the *aruvamanai*, the *molaga* (chilli) *bajji*, the catch 22 type water bottle.

Persons: CVK, Amma (my mother), Appa (my father), Kripa (my spouse), Ananya (my daughter), Samyukta (my niece), Thara (my sister), Meera (my sister), Kaushik (my son).

Activities: Chatting, mother's enquiry, half sitting-half lying posture, watching movie, buying and handing over *molaga bajji*, desperately looking for water, drinking it.

Interactions: My chatting on office matters and his health and tiredness.

Outcomes: CVK feels relaxed, rested and recovered. I am a bit embarrassed but feel alright in the end for a meaningful engagement.

Emotions: Fatigue, embarrassment, appreciation for the direct method of cure.

Environment: Overall warm, informal and friendly environment.

Interpretation

In real life, I have made a request to my company to give me a day or two off in a week for me to pursue my passions. I did this after much hesitation and almost half-heartedly. (It was a 'catch-22' situation.) It hurt my pride to make such a request and put everyone in an embarrassing position. The other reason for this hesitation is that lots of load will fall on the team mates working for me. They are already stretched and I have sometimes felt that they are not taking care of themselves.

This dream is about this dilemma I am facing in the present moment in my wake state. How?

Free Associating

Ganesha statue, the smaller one: (We pray to Ganesha and seek his blessings before we start anything.) Earlier this day, I forgot to bow/pray to this small statue and have felt I was taking *panga* (mess with or get into an issue with someone). The reference to VC Garden is because of another residue the previous late evening when my spouse helped me with my Facebook settings. I showed her my contacts and spoke about each one of them, including another schoolmate Smitha, who lived a few houses away in the same street. I had considered walking to their house and socializing but could not bring myself. I wanted to talk about it to my spouse but once again restrained myself. In our school reunion 25 years later, we both talked about it, how I missed an excellent friendship all these years. The third reference was to VC Garden 1st Street, where a Swamiji of the Ramakrishna order lived, and later served as monk at Jamshedpur, where I was doing my MBA. I was carrying some things for him from the Ramakrishna mission at Mylapore, Chennai, in which library I had a window to the world. I was startled to realize that every year, 1 or 2 students heal and recover at the Ramakrishna Math (a monastic organization). I was writing this chapter on dreams, stress, well-being and this is how this element must have found its way into the dream. It also showed an earlier dilemma about my personality as a teenager—swamiji vs socialization.

L—chair, rest, Vipassana.

Water on the bed—dirt, cavity, my broken tooth, my faults.

Cavities—crater, volcano, black, dirt, 'He is ok with it' (the bed is not ok) means I wish he accepted me with my faults?

Rajini and Kamal—the latest entrants to politics and we don't know what they are up to, they have created new political dynamics in the state of Tamil Nadu. Everyone is figuring out what these all mean. CVK took all of us to the movie means he has churned the elements and introduced new dynamics. Actually, two leaders from outside have been introduced into the department.

Molaga (chilli) *bajji*—jalmudi, jubilee park, sivakumar, ganesan, Madurai, gun shooting, balloons. This recalls an incident when at Jamshedpur, I had gone to the nearby (about 20 minutes of walk) jubilee park. My friend had earlier warned about the spicyness of *jalmudi*. I ordered just this packet dismissing my friend's suggestion that Bengali's are fond of sweets and this is a Kolkata special, and how can this be spicy for me—a South Indian? The moment I put a morsel of it in my mouth, my tongue was burning with the chillies. I had no water available and had to literally run the distance to the hostel to quench the sensation. It was quite a traumatic experience. I regretted I did not listen to my friend.

SG—downcast, now beaten, regretful, sharp nose, SR (?) (SG is substitute for SR?)

'...he had to depend on his team mates for water'—means that SR had to depend on us to emerge unscathed well from his predicament.

Amma—Appa, Apparao (the association is clear; it is Apparao's overture to enable my dreams happen that we are here talking about. The Amma (mother) is a substitute for Appa as we call him; Apparao is my new boss.

Aruvamanai—grandmother, Rama (my father's student), mockery of dignity (protest against the mockery of dignity)—it mocks my dignity and shows me to be ordinary, which is why she dismissed my protests and also shows CVK in normal light as one struggling with dilemmas. It is just the way my grand-mother brought my father down as she was cutting vegetables on such an *aruvamanai*. One of his students' had slipped on her PhD work and he was pulling her up. My grandmother was with us and pulled up my father for being so strict and severe. She started about his own pranks at school and how he was almost dismissed making the whole situation both uncomfort-able and funny.

Cutting vegetables—useful, cooking, fish, fishy (latent thought is cutting fish).
    This brings back another childhood memory. I practiced tennis and on that particular day, the coach was not ok with our playing as it had rained and the ground was wet. In exaspera-tion, much against his advice we started playing cricket with the tennis ball at the outer court. I had just swung a wild shot and was in search of the ball when I noticed that it had entered a hut in the slum nearby. I went to fetch it when I realized that the ball had broken the pot of rice that was boiling. The lady pointed it out and said, 'I am going to be beaten now by my husband for this. 'Never mind, I will manage it,' she said. I felt terribly guilty.

Blankets—What was taken away from me at the arrival of my sister—the black blanket (infantile material).... I gave him means.... I became warm to him despite my inner feelings.

Book shelf—What it alludes to is the lucky objects on top of it, the golden ship that connotes voyage, adventure and wealth, the Buddha which connotes resolution of inner conflicts and the glass and the light which connote reflection and happiness in the study of self.

Substitution

CVK symptomatically resembled NS who is stretching himself to the point of breakdown of health. He resembled the other Ganesha to whom I did not pray. At another instance, his posture resembled my former driver whose Facebook request I did not accept. The whole thing is about why I am not engaging with them on my plans. I can still release the stress of these individuals even in an alternate arrangement. I wished to give NS some rest. I admire his sincere and direct approach to things. I was embarrassed about how the switch (the change) I had sought in my working arrangement would be perceived by him.

Similarly, the substitution of SR with SG was a moment of insight. At just one angle, it was apparent that it was really SR the dream was alluding to. SR is a great friend and I do not want him seen getting hurt. I must admit that I felt he was playing 'hard to get' on what the organization was asking him to do. Seniors were asking him to take up more responsibilities. He was stretching it for a tad longer and did tell him that he is not doing the right thing. As I was advising him, I felt he was taking the advice and me lightly. The dream cleverly substituted SR so that it passed the filters of my superego whose stance is 'how can you wish a hard lesson on a friend just because he did not listen to you?' At the same time, the dream 'realized' the wish that what I had predicted has after all happened. The manifest character, SG, I had felt will rise in his career only if he learns to value others. Since he is not such a close friend, having him learn a lesson by eating 'molaga bajji' was not censored by the superego. I have wished that he learnt this lesson soon. The apparent content is the fulfilment of this wish.

At a deeper level, the dream is also asking if I am beating about the bush and playing 'hard to get' like SR about my own request for part-time working.

HAPPINE$$ MANTRA

Even a simple acknowledgement of your neurosis as revealed in your dream interpretation starts the cure of it. Yes, dream understanding constitutes at once diagnosis and therapy. This is why dream interpretation instantly leads to well-being.

Notice how I was occupying the moral high ground (lying on the cot and talking down) earlier and how I vacated this cot and struck a useful deal towards the end of the dream.

Message of the dream for my well-being:

> Leave your pretenses, shyness and create bandwidth for leadership, else you will be given a shock and cut down to size: They are ready to accept you with your faults (cavities). They both (CVK and Appa) need some rest and a place to park their troubles and take rest. You could be that solution.

—is what the dream is trying to tell me.

Should we listen to our dreams and make decisions?

Ann Faraday has spent decades in recollecting, recording and interpreting the dreams of herself and others. This is her answer to 'if our dreams are always right'.

'It is not necessary that these suggestions from the unconscious are always right. They do tell us in which direction our inner happiness lies.'

I would recommend that you subject your dream message to the test of universal distortions. If they pass the test, accept the message. You are likely to take a better decision. Ann Faraday calls this tapping dream power. Why it works is that our unconscious is allowed to ideate and generate options in an uninhibited manner and present them in dreams.

Happy dreaming!

HAPPINESS MANTRA

In case your dream apparently has no reference to a current dilemma, try pro-lucid technique of free association. You begin from what appears to you to be a most promising and adjacent element in the dream content to your wake state dilemma and produce chains of free association gently towards that dilemma. An alternative strategy would be to produce chains of free association from the salient elements in your wake state dilemma. Then see if the chains criss-cross and probe these areas. This is where the resolution is likely to be found.

8

My Body as a Well-being Compass

What can the scan of our bodies tell us about our well-being? Can the body be reoriented to pursue well-being? With many contradicting opinions, how can we base our practices on science?

Body Language

Desmond Morris is considered a leading authority on body language. Originally an anthropologist observing animal behaviour, he relates our body language to a pre-language past. The basic emotions and functionalities of living are conveyed as body language. The pre-language expression of fear, disgust, rage, heroic resolve, love, happiness, serenity, affection and sorrow is well depicted in Bharatanatyam and other dance forms. There is universality about how our bodies convey those emotions.

This leads us to wonder if there is a similar impact of repressed emotions and internalized stresses on our bodies. In his book *The Naked Eye*, Desmond Morris documented his experiences of travelling the world, observing body language and conveying the essence of being human. He alludes to the same universality of a stressed body language. He recounts a party full of medicos. Morris observes three medicos who arrive early and begin to observe all those who troop in. They are remarking intensely amongst themselves. Curious, he befriends them and asks what they were up to. They were actually predicting the cause of death of each person who entered the room!

What was interesting was how they were predicting it. If a person's body language demeanour was tense and anxious, it is a heart attack or such cardiovascular event. Similarly, they predicted stroke if the person is tense and cunning and cancer if the person is tense and nice. Desmond Morris found the whole reasoning intriguing and his own experience of the deaths of his near and dear seemed to agree with this crude prognosis of the cause of death.

One can argue that the diagnostics of medicine is in fact the observation of body language. Suppressed and repressed stressors of life—whether they are physical (like a bacterial infection) or mental (like a recent loss of job) or psychosomatic (a physical ailment that causes sleep deprivation leading to mental stress)—manifest in the way patients carry themselves. This in fact was the inspiration of Arthur Conan Doyle's *Sherlock Holmes*. Arthur Conan Doyle is inspired by a doctor who is so observant that he is able to guess the life histories of the patients he meets. He created a character called Sherlock Holmes, who of course was a detective with just this observant eye. The rest is history!

If our stressors, illnesses and conditions of life affect the way we carry our bodies, is the opposite true? Does the way we carry our bodies impact our well-being? Behaviour modifies attitudes within set limits discovered Festinger and Carlsmith. In an experiment, they asked college students to complete a boring task that lasted for a full one hour. The students' self-assessment of the experiment as boring was confirmed from them. As the experiment was over and students were about to leave, they made a special request to the students. Since their assistant was on leave, if the students could function as their assistant. All they had to do was persuade more college students to go through the experiment. To one group of students a substantial $20 of reward was given and to the other a meagre $1 was given to assist in this task. After assistance, once again the students were asked how interesting the task was. Those who had been given $20 still rated it uninteresting. Surprisingly, those who got just $1 rated the experiment they went through as interesting. They would have to otherwise admit a bitter reality to themselves. Are they so mean that for a meagre $1 they had cheated their fellow students to an uninteresting task? This dissonance between whom they think they are, decent and ethical people, versus what they did, cheat fellow students for a meagre $1, modified their attitudes. They had to now tell themselves and believe that their task was interesting. This dissonance can lead us to form bad habits. The same dissonance can be used to acquire a better sense of self and higher well-being.

Amy Cuddy did just this. The central idea is that our body language not only affects how others perceive us but even how we perceive ourselves. She calls it power posing. When we sit or stand small, slouching almost wanting to vanish, our self-assessment would be similar. We will value ourselves lesser. We need permission of those in front even to do something. We will see ourselves less free and believe it. On the other hand, when we expand ourselves, stand erect, with hands on hips or arms stretched behind or above our heads, we take up space and dominate the social dynamics. It is not only the others who respond to this expansive body language, acknowledging our dominant status; it is also ourselves who respond to this body language. We simply adopt a more resourceful and in-control attitude to life and to its challenges. Some studies have even shown that even a 2-minute adoption of an expansive posture increases our testosterone (the hormone associated with dominance and risk-taking) and reduces our cortisol (the hormone associated with stress). From the base levels, high power posing reduced cortisol by 25% while the low power poses increased cortisol by 15%.

At 19 years, Amy met with a massive car accident which led to a big head injury. She had to withdraw from college. Her IQ had dropped by 30 points. She was told that she won't be able to complete college. She worked hard and plodded to complete college. She had to take 4 more years to finish college. She ended up at Princeton feeling like an impostor. It is at this juncture that one of her mentors taught her to change her body language and feel powerful and worthy. She did the same to another student of hers. She is now convinced that body language impacts us. We change in response to our body language. Our bodies and how we express ourselves with our bodies can lead us to well-being.

My good friend, a senior person in an FMCG major, recounts his overwhelming career moment. For the first time, he had to present a due diligence outcome for a potential acquisition to a group full of seniors. This was the first time he was making such an analysis. His nightmare was if he overlooked an obvious fact and came to untenable conclusions. His seniors could judge him adversely and this could jeopardize his career. Since the nature of the transaction was of utmost confidentiality, he could not even talk to friends and seek help. He wanted to compare notes with them and figure out how his output was going to be judged. What questions and analysis he might have overlooked?

He took stock of his body language as he walked into the room. He realized he was walking tentatively. Picking himself up, he told himself that what he did was what he did. He could at least stand firm like a strong-rooted tree and speak what he found. Within a minute, he could see himself speaking with a rare confidence and conviction.

Desmond Morris discovered this quite a while ago. A man with rounded shoulders, however knowledgeable and accomplished, will take more time to the win the respect of the group he has walked into. An erect person will win our respect much easily. We are all not conscious of it, but all the same, we respond to each other and ourselves non-verbally.

So, what is the gait of the happy man, the wise man and the one who is well? How does he carry himself? Such a question was posed by Arjuna to Krishna in the Indian epic of Mahabharata. How does a man of steady wisdom walk, talk, eat?

Let us similarly reflect, understand, imitate and become a man or woman of well-being!

HAPPINESS MANTRA

Act, Become. Try and internalize appropriate body language for each occasion. It will, in turn, foster the appropriate attitude and make you the right person.

Biochemical Markers of Well-being

What are the biochemical markers when you feel well? Four biochemicals—dopamine, oxytocin, serotonin and endorphins—mark our well-being.

Dopamine gets triggered in anticipation of success. It is called the 'reward' molecule. To get a dopamine high, be outward looking, set goals and achieve them. Anticipating your vacation can trigger dopamine release. Celebrating milestones as a team releases dopamine.

Oxytocin is the 'bonding molecule'. It is triggered in the company of friends and other trusted partners. This was used by evolution to elicit cooperative behaviour amongst human beings. Hugging someone triggers the secretion of oxytocin.

Endorphin is the 'pain killing' molecule. It is produced by the pituitary gland during strenuous physical exertion like in cardio or strength training. It has also been produced by acupuncture treatment. Endorphin triggers the restful sleep and repair after a hard day of meaningful, non-anxious physical activity.

Serotonin is also called the confidence or self-esteem molecule. We can increase serotonin in our body by challenging ourselves to accomplish tasks that are difficult as well as worthwhile.

Scientist Christopher Bergland, in *The Athlete's Way*, extols simple lifestyle choices to release these happiness neurochemicals.

Other than the aforementioned four, three more cause us to feel well.

'Endocannabinoids', also called the bliss molecule, is responsible for a sense of bliss. Sustained running produces endocannabinoids in human beings and dogs. Originally, the 'runners' high' was associated with endorphin, but is now proven to be endocannabinoid.

GABA is an anti-anxiety molecule. It slows down the firing of neurons and creates a sense of calmness. GABA can be naturally increased by meditation, yoga or relaxation techniques. Medically, it is prescribed as a sedative and anti-anxiety medication.

Adrenaline or the energy molecule is the antidote to boredom. The rush of energy makes you feel alive and alert. It is also associated with an increase in heart rate, blood pressure and muscle contraction.

In the Silicon Valley at the USA there are a group of people experimenting a biochemical approach to health, well-being and even intelligence and success. This is the bio-hacking movement. They use the techniques of science, the powers of modern medical testing and their own subjective observations to dramatically alter their moods, health and IQ. They also share information with each other about their experiments and results so that others can avoid personal trials and errors. A team of doctors, psychologists and experts support these bio-hackers.

For example, consider a parameter like the 'wear and tear' of our bodies. This is what we call as ageing. Every time you eat food and go about the business of life, your body oxidizes. When iron oxidizes you call it rusting. When a cut apple oxidizes, the brown coat it acquires is like the apple going bad. When fuel oxidizes, we call it burning. All of them have a natural ending point when they can oxidize no further as useful content is exhausted. In biological terms when our bodies acquire free radicals, or oxidative ions in technical terms, we grow old and eventually die. At the cellular level, this is expressed by a genetic material called teleomere. The shorter our teleomeres, the closer the cells are to their death. Cells die and are replaced all the time. Even in these replaced new cells, shorter teleomeres mean ageing. As cells age, their ability to faithfully copy a replacement reduces. When cells copy incorrectly, we call it cancer. As the cells of an organ grow old in the manner described above, the organ malfunctions. A malfunctioning organ in turn affects other organs starting a vicious cycle of decay and death. For example, a malfunctioning kidney is no longer able to remove the impurities from the body. These impurities poison the system and in turn causes other organs like the liver to malfunction. A malfunctioning brain introduces rapid deterioration in the functioning of the individual.

Our bodies are beautifully designed to self-heal, within limits. When we are younger, this self-healing system works well. Some other system is able to take the stress of the malfunctioning area, fight it and restore the original balance. Infection is fought by fever; poor blood circulation to the brain is fought by increasing our blood pressure and so on. The self-healing system can quickly break down when the person does not have enough and good quality sleep.

But, can we slow down this wear and tear? When bears hibernate during winters, go without food and water, they practically shut down their bodies and repair themselves. For all practical purposes, the bear does not age during the period of hibernation. Even when we sleep, our body slows down. Our blood pressure drops, pulse rate drops, breathing slows down and so do brain activities. This slowing down is why you are able to go on for 8 hours of sleep without feeling hungry. In the waking state, we would feel hunger every four hours. Even when you get up, it takes a while before you start feeling hungry. Our sugar levels and the energy available to work do reduce, but not very dramatically. This is the reason for measuring fasting sugar in the testing for diabetes.

Returning to our original question, can we age slower? By adapting a different mechanism in the way our foods digest and energy gets produced, we can slow ourselves down. Dietologists and biologists call this the ketosis mechanism versus the glycolysis that most of us use to supply energy to ourselves. In ketosis, the stored fat of the body is utilized to release energy. In glycolysis, the stored glucose is utilized to produce energy. Ketosis produces 3 units of energy for every such digestive reaction compared to one unit in the case of glycolysis.

Almost all of us get our energy from the breakdown of glucose in the body and this glucose is supplied by the carbohydrates in our diet. This is far less efficient than the burning of fat. Practices like fasting trigger the burning of fat. This is perhaps the reason for several religious practices based on fasting. It is like efficient burning of fuel that produces no smoke versus inefficient burning that produces lots of smoke and dirt. In certain diets, people are asked to eat only a richly fat diet—65% fat, 30% protein and 5% minerals, vitamins and carbohydrates. They also eat only once in 24 hours. Initially, this can be inconvenient, but after a week our bodies adapt to this input. After a month of adjustment, people have reported marked increases in their focus, energy and concentration. They also report health improvements, immunity to fight infection, quality of sleep, etc. Surprisingly, there is no craving or hunger. A mouth odour and a certain fruity smell to our urine signify the transition of the body from glycolysis to ketosis as the primary energy mechanism. By contrast, processed and sugary drinks are the most inefficient energy supply mechanisms and they wear our bodies much faster. This is the reason for the age-old advice asking us to eat fruit instead of processed sugar. Prior to our transition to agriculture, ketosis supplied energy to our prehistoric ancestors. Scientists hypothesize that this was the era of excellent health and happiness for us. We were killed by predators certainly. We did not suffer from infections and certainly not from lifestyle diseases. When we go backpacking into deep forests and mountains, we are yearning to live this very lifestyle.

At this point in our history, we had tamed the fire. So we could cook the meat we hunted, boil the fish and vegetables we could lay our hands on. We cooperated with each other to feed ourselves a high fat and high protein diet once a day. Cooking softened the food and helped our brains grow larger in size. The average human brain is 2% of the body weight but consumes 20% of the energy. To feed our growing brains, we had to be chewing all day long. It is the fire that softened the food; made sure we did not have to eat all day, provided energy and helped our brains grow in size. Our growing brains and free time is the catalyst of our evolution, of you, me and our pursuit of happiness.

HAPPINESS MANTRA

Mindfully observe the impact of actions and food on your bodies. Experiment and discover your well-being protocol of eating, moving and sleeping. Do consult your physician before you undertake any extreme experiments.

This era, biochemically as well as psychodynamically, is one milestone of well-being. We cooperated, released oxytocin. We walked about a nomadic existence releasing endorphins to block the pain of walking barefoot in thick jungles. When we got a catch we released dopamine and when we ran wildly, endo-cannabinoids. As we made complex tools, we were awash with serotonin. We aged slower as we gave ourselves energy through ketosis, the more efficient mechanism. Surely, we could fall prey to predators but the powerful fire that we had tamed gave us great advantages and security. The social structure was not pervasive and did not dominate our lives. We did not have a large superego to make us feel small and guilty. Recall how social injunctions get internalized as our superego. Our id was slowly refined by the reality of life and our new-found ability to think and express. We did not settle down as we did post agriculture to compare the sizes of our huts and feel envious. We were moderately bored. We did not have nervous excitement of doing too much and neither did we suffer from a melancholic emptiness as survival itself was an interesting project. This was perhaps the happiest point we achieved as humans.

The interested reader can explore the impact of social organization on our primal well-being by reading *Civilization and its Discontents* by Sigmund Freud.

Blue Zones and Longevity

In the modern world, where the fear of predators is dramatically reduced, can longevity be a marker for well-being? When a group of people live longer than others, does that mean their bodily wear and tear is slower? Do they age at lesser rates? Can we study them to understand useful protocols for well-being?

Yes, places where the percentage of people who live to a 100+ years is highest are blue Zones. Sardinia (Italy), Okinawa (Japan), Nicoya (Costa Rica), Icaria (Greece) and among the Seventh-day Adventists in Loma Linda, California, USA, are the blue zones of the world.

Dan Buettner publicized these regions in a National Geographic cover story in 2005. He studied the common characteristics of these peoples. He wanted to reverse engineer longevity. Here are a few lessons he learnt from the lifestyle of the blue zoners.

Moderate, Regular Physical Activity

You will be surprised that most of the blue zones people do not exercise! To be precise, they do not do intentional exercise. Their lifestyle ensured that they have to move about, get up and down from the floor. Folks who exercise every day and look at their tummies and wonder why it has not come down are doing more harm than good. They are undertaking physical activity in an anxious state of mind. The way blue zones people exercise is by listening to their bodies. Exercise is a by-product of a thoughtful lifestyle. It is not a tick in the box or activity on our timetable that can make us guilty if we did not do it!

On the blue zones model, the chief of Albert Lea of Minnesota redesigned life in this place by focusing on the ecology of health. Instead of asking individuals to adapt a blue zone lifestyle, he redesigned public spaces and prompters to adapt this lifestyle. On the major predictors of health, Albert Lea showed dramatic improvements. City officials reported a

40% reduction in healthcare costs. If predictive statistics are to be believed, the people of Albert Lea added 3 good years to their life expectancy.

Life Purpose

'Ikigai' is a neat Japanese conception of life purpose. Loosely translated, it means the reason to live. The long-lived blue zoners from Okinawa, Japan, see this as a central concept to their lives. When one has found their Ikigai, there is no longer any strain in any striving. The actions are spontaneous and what you are doing is the most natural thing to do. Usually, an Ikigai is a cause larger than oneself. Usually Ikigai is when we are working on our strengths. The concept of flow—the neurobiology of excellence by Mihaly Csikszentmihalyi is very similar.

Victor Frankl in his famous book, *Man's Search for Meaning'* alludes to this Ikigai. Victor Frankl was caught by the Germans during the Second World War and sent to a Nazi concentration camp. His Ikigai was to complete his research quest and convey it to the world. He would write on pieces of paper and stitch them onto his coat, bear countless brutalities so he could complete the project. Many freedom fighters endured their painful jail terms because they had a reason to live. Recently, I had been to the cell that Veer Savarkar stayed for 10 long years at Andaman. The jail itself, called 'Kala Pani' indicated that when one reached here, one never went out except after dying. Savarkar was given a cell that overlooks the hanging spot for convicts to break him down mentally. He was given a rationed amount of food and water and brutal physical labour. The inmates had to squeeze coconut oil more than what a bull would be flogged to do every day. It was Ikigai that made Savarkar attempt a near-successful escape. It was Ikigai that helped him endure the hardships and shine like an intellectual. Those 10 years could have broken anyone, but not Savarkar.

Even when you are not living under exceptional circumstances, you can find your Ikigai by experimentation and self-analysis. It is not necessary for your Ikigai to be lofty. To a Japanese woman at 102 years, holding her great, great, great granddaughter was the Ikigai.

The blue zoners also had a marked preoccupation with spirituality and religion.

Stress Reduction

The idea of a complete switch-off is very central to the blue zones. The Seventh-day Adventists of Loma Linda devote one day of the week to nature walks. Such a complete switch-off reverses the inflammatory response in the body. Some countries such as Denmark and Netherlands have corporate practices to not deliver electronic email when someone is on vacation! The server sends a standard response stating that 'so and so is on vacation and hence this email has not been transmitted. Please resend after such and such a date'. Denmark and Netherlands have figured amongst the happiest countries in the world consecutively for 4 years. No wonder!

Diet

It takes about 30 minutes for the gut to tell the brain that it is full. People who eat fast are likely to overeat. The centenarians of Okinawa in Japan have three strategies to moderate their calories intake and prevent overeating. Firstly, they eat on small plates. Secondly, they pick up food from a central table but go to their corners to eat their food. They do not indulge in the munching-talking cycle in a mindless way. Thirdly, they sit on the floor on their knees and bend down to eat. The moment the stomach becomes full, it becomes stressful to bend the body to eat further. They use these signals to subtly remind themselves to moderate their calories.

A 95% plant-based diet characterized the blue zones people. They also moderated their alcohol intake. They had a glass of wine high in resveratrol. Resveratrol prevents cellular inflammation and is suspected to have even anti-ageing benefits. Nuts such as pistachio, peanuts; grapes, red and white wine are high on resveratrol.

Pro-social Focus

A strong engagement to family and their well-being characterized blue zone cultures. Family came first as a big value system. These were also places where the older people were respected and accepted for their wisdom or simply for their affection.

Amongst the Okinawa women, there is a concept of moai. These are typically group of 5 or 6 people who commit to a lifelong friendship with each other. They will be there for them when one of them goes through a rough patch in life. Some of the moai's are operational for 90+ years amongst these 100-year old women. The realization that you are part of a moai gives an immense sense of security and well-being.

Positive psychologist Martin Seligman says if you have a friend that you can comfortably call at 3:30 AM in the morning, you have a higher chance of mental health, happiness and longevity. This is the comfort and security that the culture of a moai, a lifetime of committed friendship, gives a human being.

HAPPINESS MANTRA

Compare your lifestyle with the blue zoners. Find out what changes you can immediately make to align and make them. Do you move about enough and without anxiety? Do you eat till you are 3/4ths full? Do you have an Ikigai? Do you have a moai? Do you have a day a week of true Sabbath where you switch off from your routine and connect with nature?

More Biological Markers

We contemplated how body language changes our bio-chemistry. Pro-social behaviours dramatically alter our biochemistry too. To be precise, the relationship is two-way, the right biochemistry leads to pro-social behaviours and vice versa.

It is not difficult to guess why evolution made us pro-social. Amongst all the animals, the human animal has the longest childhood relative to its lifespan. As the crow's egg hatches and a baby crow is born, in a little time, it is ready to fly. The tiger cub is ready to hunt and the cow's calf to wander about independently and take care of itself. All of them are born nearly complete. Their brains are nearly fully formed. The human head grows in circumference from infancy all the way to adulthood. Had our brains been fully formed, we would not have the freedom to internalize new behaviours based on our exposure to the world. Even practically, at that circumference, our mothers' would have to be much larger creatures introducing new problems for the human kind. Evolution created a nice device to solve this problem by making the human baby a very small creature compared to the size he/she will reach at adulthood.

This solution introduced new problems. The human infant had to be shielded, secured and nurtured for a much longer time. The family and the pair bond are a neat device to solve this problem. Only those human creatures who had a tendency to pair bond and nurture their offspring survived, pro-created. To cut a long story short, we have it in our genes to cuddle babies. We have it in our genes to cooperate to raise a family. We have it in our genes to cooperate, save each other and hunt together.

Biologically, the vagus nerve manifests several of these functions. If one has to trace a single anatomical/physiological marker for well-being, it is the vagus nerve and the vagal tone. This nerve runs across the body and mediates the functioning of several organ systems. It is unusually long and winds through our body and hence shares the common word root with vagabond— someone who wanders about.

The vagus nerve is responsible for the relaxation response. It has got sensory (communicate from body to brain) and motor (brain to body) fibres. It mediates the functioning of the heart, lungs and the digestive tract and indirectly several parts of the body.

It makes our breath deep, long and steady creating an internal ambience of calmness. A higher vagal tone means higher oxytocin and lower cortisol. It also increases our digestive juices. Gastrointestinal disorders are hugely influenced by stress response. It helps break down fat into energy in a more efficient way. By regulating insulin, it achieves a steady equilibrium of blood sugar. Fluctuating sugar levels or higher levels of blood sugar increases the body wear and tear. It improves heart rate variability (HRV).

HRV is now becoming a central marker for present and future health. When we take an in-breath, our heart rate is faster and at the out breath, slower. In healthy people, there is a good variation in the heart rate with each sinus cycle. Those with poor cardiovascular health or prognosis seem to have lower heart rate variability.

Anxious children stimulate their vagal response by pursing their lips and blowing through their mouths. As their lips vibrate at this manoeuvre, producing a shrill sound, they activate their parasympathetic or calming response.

The diver's high—as a diver jumps into water, head down is actually a vagal response. This is one of the reasons why playing in water or swimming is so calming and refreshing. The vagus nerve gets stimulated when cold water splashes on our face.

There are 32 ways to stimulate the vagus nerve! Do consult your doctor before doing any of these physical manoeuvres. However, pro-social behaviours can increase your vagal tone without any dangers.

Cultivating Pro-social Behaviours

In her article 'The biology of kindness', Maia Szalavitz documents several benefits of a pro-social outlook. Maia is a neuroscience journalist at Time.com. She quotes studies which show that strong relationships have as much benefit as avoiding smoking and obesity. 65 people were recruited for this study. Half of them were assigned to a class on loving kindness meditation while the other half were not. Both the groups were asked to document their positive and negative emotions as well as the meditation they did. In the class, the group was first taught to contemplate their own worries and slowly expand to include others in their social contacts. They mentally repeated phrases wishing these others well. The heart rate variability was tested for all before and after this 6 week intervention. The meditating group showed an overall increase in joy, amusement, serenity and hope. Along with these psychological changes, the vagal tone and the heart rate variability also improved in the meditating group. This group had tuned themselves to become more pro-social. There were two further insights from this study. Simply meditating did not improve these health markers. Only if the emotions turned positive and they became more pro-social the vagal tone improved. The second outcome was that those who already had a higher vagal tone improved even higher.

Jon Kabat Zinn, the molecular biologist from MIT is credited with bringing mindfulness meditation to mainstream medicine and stress reduction. He describes mindfulness as wise and affectionate attention. He designed an 8 week course on mindfulness-based stress reduction.

He found that the pre-frontal cortex activation shifted from right to left in the volunteers. The right side pre-frontal cortex in the brain lights up when a person is anxious, fearful, wants to avoid the experience. The left side lights up when the person is relaxing, calm and happy. When a flu shot was administered to the experimental and control group, those trained in mindfulness-based stress reduction had a better immune response. Also, regions of the brain important for learning, memory, decision-making and perspective thickened while regions responsible for the fight or flight response, the amygdale thinned. Dr Zinn was himself amazed at the amount of structural changes in the brain that mindfulness practices introduced.

He says parenting—a source of stress—can be an excellent mindfulness practice. It exercises your pro-social best. You are programmed for it. If you are savouring every moment with your children—calmly, affectionately, wisely, mindfully—you are doing a great deal of good to yourself and them.

Compassion Temple Exercise

If you are religious and go to a place of worship, you are likely to be reflective. The ritual of entering the temple allows you to suspend your worries. It allows you to observe, pray. Usually, people go to a place of worship to resolve to complete certain things and ask for divine help. The next time you are at a place of worship, try something else.

Fix your attention on a stranger, someone you may not meet again. It could be a child, an old man or woman, a pregnant lady, anyone. Like all of us, visualize that they too have come to the temple with some wishes. Add your prayers to their prayers. Focus this visit on asking divine help for their wish. Ring the bell after they have prayed. Genuinely try to wish them well mentally. Wish that their dreams come true sooner than later. Wish them success, happiness in their pursuit. Tell yourself that this one visit is not about you, but them. By empathizing with others and extending the zone of compassion to someone whom you may not meet, you will notice a well-spring of good feelings. Your hands have become warmer. Your breathing is easy and steady. You switch to a great mood. You feel secure. You have activated the biology of kindness.

HAPPINESS MANTRA

Undertake the compassion temple exercise once a week or at least once a fortnight.

Collective Prayer

Praying together activates physiological and biochemical changes. The sense of common purpose and common community gets activated. You belong and it is a milder version of the moai. At this juncture, should you be stuck by some emergency, you are more likely to receive help. The rhythmic humming of the prayer activates a para-sympathetic response in itself. The collective, co-operative behaviour releases oxytocin. God is a parent substitute, minus their flaws. It increases our sense of security and produces a calming response.

HAPPINESS MANTRA

Do a collective act for the greater good every fortnight. Engage in collective praying or singing.

Gratitude

Gratitude is the complement to compassion. By feeling grateful and not taking the kind acts of others for granted, you can increase your sense of well-being. The gratitude journal is one of the most popular activities in courses on well-being and happiness. Every day in the morning and at night, you are asked to recollect three things that you are grateful for and three people you are grateful to. Doing this for only 21 days produces noticeable subjective states of well-being. You are less anxious and calmer even in the face of stressful situations.

HAPPINESS MANTRA

Recollect three events that you are grateful for every night and three people you are grateful for every morning.

Mental Subtraction and Savouring

Mental subtraction is not taking even the simple things for granted. In mental subtraction, you mentally dispossess yourself of even core things such as your arms and legs. You open your eyes to feel blessed that you have them.

The other deliberate exercise we are taught to practice is savouring. This is to be in the present moment totally. The popular advice to 'slow down and smell the roses' is in fact an advice to savour. In many countries, people have embraced the slow life movement. Their internet speeds are slow, their eating is slow.

In a popular mindfulness exercise, experts teach us to savour a raisin. The following is adapted from the Greater Good Science Center at the University of Berkley. The University of Berkley has them adapted from the works of Teastdale, Segal and Zinn.

First, take a raisin and hold it in the palm of your hand (holding). Take your time to fully focus on it. Imagine that it dropped from the sky and you are seeing this for the first time (seeing). Turn the raisin with your fingers, exploring its texture. Maybe do this with your eyes closed to enhance your sense of touch (touching). Take the raisin near your nose and try to smell it. With each in-breath notice any aroma that may be there (smelling). Now, slowly bring the raisin to your lips noticing how you do it perfectly. Spend a few moments on the sensations it is creating on your tongue (placing). When you are ready, start chewing the raisin. Notice how it is at the right place for you to chew. Notice an early taste sensation and the subsequent changes in taste as you extract the juice off the raisin (tasting). When you are ready to swallow, notice how the intention to swallow arises. After noticing the intent, gently swallow the raisin (swallowing). Do see if you can follow the raisin as it leaves your mouth all the way to your stomach (following).

HAPPINESS MANTRA

Undertake mindful eating 5 minutes a day, every day.

Switching off and savouring are back in fashion. Amongst the intellectual elites in California, several live in a zone where no internet or mobile phone works. Did you know that the land prices have shot up there because of this unique facility?

9

Meditation: Why, When and How It Works?

Our bodies mediate the exchange of material between the external world and ourselves. The body is our outermost layer. We ingest food, air, water and other sensory inputs like touch, smell, sound, sight and taste. By the inputs themselves or by our interpretation and in turn by our reaction and response, we feel well or miserable.

Meditation is an inward journey and starts where the body stops. Ultimately, it is a contemplation of oneself. It is an exploration of our identity and our place in the world. In meditation, we try to minimize sensory input and focus on how we process any input. By improving awareness of how we process, meditation provides clarity on how we engage with the world. From this awareness, we can choose to make this engagement productive. Meditation creates a buffer zone where we can experience the self without the world. It creates a buffer zone that for a moment shuts out how the world has dealt with us. It explores how we deal with ourselves.

Genetic predispositions, early experiences and memories form a smokescreen that permanently colour how we view the world. The transactional analysts generalized this phenomenon as our life position. Each layer of the smokescreen attracts more smoke as we go through life. The transactional analysts said that we act to confirm our life positions. The screen gets thicker and our view of the world becomes more distorted. The world also becomes familiar. A point is reached when we only see the smokescreen and no longer see the world. This is the point of mental breakdown.

By observing this smokescreen as a generator of input, by understanding how it operates, we attempt to clear it. Meditation de-fogs our window to the world. It makes our view of the world real, novel, amusing and vivid with all its faults and wonders. Meditation is an examination of our filters to the world.

HAPPINESS MANTRA

The goal of meditation is to understand our own smoke-screens and discount them.

Types of Meditation

No two people can meditate alike. Meditation itself passes through the very filters it is seeking to clear. The methods that we employ are what we are talking of as the types of meditation. There are numerous brands of meditation around these methods. We have Vipassana, Sudarshan Kriya, Chakra, Kundalini, Zen, Mindfulness, Japa, Transcendental and Vichara just to name a few. There are many thousands of followers for each one of them.

Meditation is performed in various postures. One can be sitting cross-legged, or even in Padmasana, sitting with your knees and feet underneath, sitting comfortably in a chair or lying down on your back. Meditation is rarely practiced standing up. The act of balancing ourselves on two feet is a pretty complex one. It distracts us from the exploration of the self and the filters. One does not meditate face down either. The diaphragm as we breathe pushes against the bed and creates its own distracting sensations.

Often, meditation is performed with eyes closed as sight is a powerful sensory input. Light and sight can distract us from the exploration of oneself. Similarly, meditation is performed amidst mild positive fragrances. When our eyes are closed and we have smells, our limbic brain wonders what the smell is all about. This again distracts us from self-exploration. For the same reason, meditation is not practised amidst loud sound or when the ambient temperature is too cold or hot. Meditation is not performed when one is tired and sleepy and certainly not in the lying down position! The *Visuddhimagga* is an elaborate Buddhist text on meditation. Hundreds of pages have been devoted in this text on the ambience of meditation.

The different forms of meditation differ from each other on their starting point. The anchor point of the inward journey can either be the bodily reactions, the breath, thoughts and feelings, self-observation at the instance of apprehending an external object or a direct reflection on our identity. In Sanskrit, these starting points are codified as layers of being. The layers are Annamaya Kosa (the physical), Pranamaya Kosa (the vital), Manomaya Kosa (the mental), Vijnanamaya Kosa (the rational) and Anandamaya Kosa (the spiritual).

Vipassana

In Vipassana, the inward journey starts at the physical–vital boundary. The initial content of the meditation is the physiology and mechanics of respiration. The initial goal of this focus is to make respiration fully conscious.

Both the Hindus and the Buddhists were practitioners of Vipassana. In the Bhagavad Gita, Krishna says, 'Amongst meditations, I am Vipassana'. The yogic method of being conscious of posture (the *asanas*) and breathing (*pranayama*) alludes to this physical–vital starting point. Yoga and Pranayama focus on bodily mechanisms that are semi-conscious, controlled by the cerebellum in our brains. Yogic postures try to alter our body chemistry. The face lock amidst the collar bones in Sarvangasana activates the thyroid gland for instance. If you practice the Halasana, you can feel your pulse slowing down. Amongst the cobblers in India is the lowest incidence of kidney disease, and it is correlated to the way they sit to perform their work— the Baddha Konasana. How yogic poses alter body chemistry and in turn impact our moods and health is a vast book by itself. The Buddhists are also credited with the Vipassana. The Buddha was certainly a master practitioner of Vipassana. The Buddha it is said had such vivid awareness of his body that he once set a dislocated bone back in its place.

You typically start observing your breathing. It does not matter if your breath is short. It does not matter if it is shallow. Equally, it does not matter if it is long and deep. You are to merely observe your breath. If there are other bodily sensations crying for your attention, observe them. You will soon get thought associations. They can be around your breath, or your body sensations. Gently bring it back to your breath. You may be able to observe the breath as it gets in through the nostrils all the way to your diaphragm. Your focus may shift to how your diaphragm rises and falls with each breathing cycle. There could be thought associations around the calm feeling produced by such observation. You would soon be following those associations and trains of thought. As you notice that you have wandered, gently bring the attention back to your breathing again. When in doubt, bring it specifically to the tip of your nostrils as air enters your body. Focus on the region between your nose tip and lips. Notice the sensations in the region. Gently, bring it back to your breathing again.

You will soon notice your breath becoming longer, steadier and effortless. Do this for 20 minutes or 40 minutes or as much you feel comfortable. As the breath becomes longer and steadier, there is a tendency to sustain it. Resist this sensation to force a long and steady breathing. By controlling, directing you are moving away from a meditative state. As you try to control and direct, you will notice that it no longer feels pleasant and comfortable. Once again accept your short and shallow breaths. You will automatically notice your body relaxing. The sensations of the body that cried for attention have become fewer and farther. If they do return, don't get anxious. Just watch them. Accept them. Don't follow them. Don't wish more of it or less of it. Take it just the way it is.

You need to be comfortably seated so that the body is naturally balanced. There is no strain to balance. Your spinal column is one on top of another and hence balanced effortlessly. This ensures that lesser body sensations are produced. You can also do this lying down on your back. The strain of balancing is overcome in a lying posture.

The Buddhists also recommend we bring the heart into the meditation. One has to feel grateful for being alive. The life causes the breath not the other way round as Swami Vivekananda says. Watch your breath with tender curiosity just like the way the Gorilla watches over its kids.

This is Vipassana meditation.

Why Does It Lead to Well-being?

The physiological and psychological processes triggered by this meditation are fascinating. Lehrer and Gevirtz discuss a certain cardiorespiratory biofeedback training to improve heart rate variability in the journal, frontiers of psychology. With the help of instruments giving feedback to us on our biorhythms, they help participants achieve high heart rate variability and peak amplitudes. They achieve resonance between the different systems of the body. We will simplify this study for our readers and relate it to the Vipassana type of meditation.

The lungs expand as we take an in-breath and through gas exchange at the alveoli oxygenate the blood. The oxygen-rich blood is pumped to all parts of the body. When blood oxygen is at its highest, the pulse rate and blood pressure raise providing oxygen and nutrients to different cells in the body. The nerves in turn provide the electric signals for the heart to beat. The frequency and intensity of the signals are a factor in the pulse rate and blood pressure, respectively. Another mechanism called the baroreflex, the stretching level of arteries, in turn, causes the blood pressure to fall. In individuals with peak health, these systems are perfectly tuned to each other. When they are tuned to each other, high amplitudes are reached for the sinus rhythm—the height of the graph an ECG draws.

When the systems are tuned, the ECG graph shows high variability of the heart rate.

Even in the so-called healthy individuals, there is a 90° phase lag between the different systems. People who are trained through biofeedback or meditative practices like Vipassana remove even this phase lag. The biomechanics of living becomes quite effortless. One can hypothesize that this would significantly reduce wear and tear, reduce the inflammatory response, improve vagal tone, increase the well-being biochemicals and improve the quality of our lives.

Most people breathe 9–24 breaths per minute. Even at resting respiratory rates, the peak heart rate is achieved at the mid-point of the in-breath and lowest heart rate is achieved at about the mid-point of the out-breath. Instead of mid-point, if we achieve at end point of the in-breath and similarly the end-point of the out-breath, the lung and pulse systems are at resonance. Based on bio-feedback training, it is found that for most people a breathing rate of 6 breaths per minute causes resonance and optimal functioning. When the heart rate starts increasing at the beginning of inhalation and peaks at the end of it, this produces the most optimum exchange of gases. This in turn induces a vagal tone and relaxation response that also regulates the nerve signals. This is moderated by signals from the brainstem and a region of the amygdala. Amygdala is the seat of stress or fight of flight response. The three-system resonance in turn creates a positive feedback loop and optimal functioning. Similarly, the optimal variation in blood pressure also occurs at a similar 5.5 or 6 breath per minute. The HRV biofeedback is utilized in medical practice to treat anxiety and depression.

At the physiological level, Vipassana achieves this perfect resonance.

Zen Meditation

In Zen meditation, the inward journey starts at the vital–mental boundary. What are gently focused upon are the thoughts and feelings that arise in the consciousness. The initial goal for this focus is to become aware of mental turbulence. We become aware of the dynamics of mentation. Thoughts and feeling clouds arise in consciousness and they pass by. We are not to follow them but merely observe. You will notice that you are subtly getting entangled and following thoughts. Every time you realize this is happening, you are to gently pull yourself back to observation. There should be no performance anxiety in Zen meditation, or any meditation for that matter. This is practice. Mistakes are part of the practice. Be gentle and kind to yourself. Forgive yourself for being entangled from time to time.

Zen meditation is similar to the techniques of free associa-tion employed by the psychoanalysts. The big difference is that in free association, dream content became a starting point and hence it directly revealed our personal complexes. Also free associated material is analysed for patterns and the attempt is to interpret them. In Zen, there is no interpretation. It is watchfully attending to thoughts and feeling as they arise in consciousness.

A point comes in the practice where you realize vividly that the thoughts and feelings that arise *are not your* conscious-ness. The screen of consciousness reflects these images and emotions but is never those images and emotions.

Transcendental Meditation

In Transcendental Meditation (TM) one focuses on an esoteric object or image or sound. For example one could focus on the sound of flowing water or 'Aum'. By bringing your atten-tion back to the same object, image or sound ad nauseam, a tipping point is reached. At this tipping point, one no longer is preoccupied with the object, image or sound but its echo and reflection in consciousness. One begins to question how we perceive the world.

TM also begins the inward journey at the mental layer.

Vichara: Inquiry into Identity

The Vichara way of self-inquiry is perhaps the most direct. The one question that permeates this inquiry is 'Who am I?' The Ramana Maharishi is the recent master practitioner of Vichara. At a young age, he began to contemplate the meaning of death. He lied down and pretended to be dead. Now, they are taking my body and consigning to flames, now my family is grieving. So, who am I?

The inquiry is somewhat similar to the philosopher Rene Descartes' doubt. He once dreamt of a butterfly and in this dream, the butterfly slept and dreamt of Descartes. After he woke up, he was not sure if this was real or if he is still acting the butterfly's dream. He was possessed with this overwhelming doubt on the certainty of his existence. After much reflection, he concluded that this inquiry itself makes him a certainty. 'I think therefore I am' was his emphatic resolution.

The Ramana Maharishi discovered that the questioner, the question and the answer are all one. It is an undivided stream of consciousness.

HAPPINESS MANTRA

Meditation ceases to be one if there is an anxiety to perform. Meditation is gentle, non-judgemental awareness that relaxes the body, calms the mind and clarifies one's place in the world.

Can Hobbies Be Meditation?

Hobbies can be meditative and lead to happiness was a profound insight from Bertrand Russell. He called them impersonal interests. Assimilating information, making decisions, anxious to get them right are part of professional career. They exercise the will and are fatiguing. It does not matter one is working in the very area one was interested in. A doctor has just become what she always wanted to be. She is now reading about the latest advances in the treatment of a disease. It is interesting and positive to her. It does not quite have the characteristic of an impersonal interest. The doctor is reading it because she can be one better than her colleagues. It has got the burden of competition in it.

Hobbies on the contrary are impersonal interests. They are done for their own sake. They may even be the minor interest of this doctor. By the way, she also wanted to try her hand at pottery or haiku. These are nothing to do with her profession. When she indulges in them, she switches off from the tensions of her work—if she will get funding, will her research get published or if she can arrange her schedule and attend that conference. A man or woman who can switch off from their work and not worry about it till they start on their work again is a happy person, says Russell. The hobbies are an excellent switch off. We are working on something that is of interest. It has got nothing to do with our main profession or career. They are being done for their own sake. There is no pressure or compulsion to retain and comprehend. This total lack of compulsion is what makes them a non-neurotic activity.

Such pursuits bring a profound calm and sagacious demeanour to us. We feel the world is fundamentally alright. Even in day-to-day life, the compulsions of society forbid us from behaving in a certain way or force us to put up a show. In the pursuit of hobbies, only the id and ego are active. Since these hobbies are not about people, the burden of messy relationships and implicit expectations are not making us anxious. This is the reason why we can stare at fish for hours. We expect nothing from the fish and the fish expects nothing from us. It is an unburdened presence amidst each other. We know that the fish does not care if we are beautiful or ugly. The id is not frustrated.

This is the same kind of absorption that Mihaly Csikszentmihalyi talks about in his book *Flow*. Our relationship with time gets altered when we are absorbed. We notice the hobby, how the pot is shaping up in an unhurried but exquisite detail. Similar to the meditative state, we achieve a detached observation. The differences between meditation and such impersonal absorption are twofold. Even as we achieve the detachment, our sense of self diminishes and almost vanishes in the case of hobbies. In meditation, it is harder to achieve this. The starting point of meditation itself is our well-being. It introduces an element of a narcissistic ego play in the equation. There are also a few rules in meditation. Try to be non-judgementally aware. Try to pull back and observe your thoughts, feelings and sensations without following them. Even if they are applied very gently, they do exercise the superego—our sense of dos and don'ts and our sense of guilt, shame and regret.

Further these interests (hobbies) widen the perspective on life. With many such interests, we can no longer be frog in the well, only seeing and measuring life in terms of a small set of colleagues. It allows us to contemplate the finiteness of our existence. It reminds us that much of our thoughts and actions which are overwhelmingly important for our good and victory are petty in the larger scheme of things. This contemplation engages the ego, our sense of reality than the superego, our sense of dos and don'ts or right and wrong. It is hence 'our' decision not to be petty. It is not the internalization of authority which is the superego.

Russell regards absorption in impersonal hobbies as even superior to meditation in the conquest of happiness.

HAPPINESS MANTRA

Having several hobbies that you pursue for its own sake is a clear antidote to unhappiness and a path to happiness.

The Common Thread

The different forms of meditation fuse into each other. Most of them describe the summit of their practice in very similar terms. The world is apprehended in our consciousness. Meditation is about apprehending this consciousness. As meditation ripens, the individual achieves an awareness of his/her transparent consciousness. The streams of experience that flow through us, the experiences of the day and even the dreams of the night are seen as distinct from our consciousness. We are able to watch without entanglement. We can even achieve a state of lucid dreaming. At lucidity, we are able to realize we are dreaming while dreaming! If we choose to, we can even redirect our dreams! At this level of mastery, we can discount the reactions that arise in ourselves, the distortions they introduce as we engage with the world. Several practitioners have reported an inner joy and peace once this transparency of consciousness is achieved. They seem to understand the place of the self in the world and achieve a universal connectedness. At this point, even their fear of death diminishes. They see death as a transformation of state not as a destruction of consciousness. A great sense of security and well-being arise at this insight. The drama of life is enjoyed, not even rationally endured from this insight onwards.

Whether the summit of the practice of meditation is a permanent happy attitude or extraordinary self-delusion is a matter of great controversy. The rationalists advance the following arguments in their favour. If the human condition is seeded with misery, rational endurance of this misery is the real summit of mastery. Courageously coping with this misery and helping others cope with it is the real heroism. The fact that one can be rational and courageous in the face of misery is the heroic excellence. Choosing to have free thoughts and individual opinions in the face of the overwhelming forces of life is the hero's journey. Happiness is the perfect response, the most rational response. As the stoics described, it is to discriminate if the matter is up to us or not up to us. If it is up to us, to act, change, control, master. If it is not up to us, endure. The same sense of discrimination of 'viveka' in Sanskrit resonates in the dialogue between Krishna and Arjuna in The Bhagavad Gita. Transcendence from this misery into oceanic bliss as described by Gurus is a project in self-delusion. It is just another type of neurosis, a collective neurosis. This neurosis is well seeded and well supported by collective guilt. The excessive preoccupation with oneself is irrational narcissism and infantile regression.

The other side argues that the dismissal of such a fine practice is motivated by prejudice. The filters of the self are examined and gently neutralized. They are not being denied. The correct practice of meditation is never to deny. Non-judgemental awareness is the very core of meditation. The inability of the rationalists to transcend their limitations does not mean they cannot be transcended. The rationalists are limited by the range of human experiences that one accesses. There is a next evolution. Can a monkey understand the fuss we make or the graceful dance of melodious music we relish? These next stages of experience are being judged harshly and prematurely.

I am no expert in the field of meditation to provide a final opinion on this matter. There are enough studies and independent experiments to show meditation increases well-being. The same bio-markers of well-being are activated by the practice of meditation.

I have practised Vipassana rather less rigorously. Sometimes focusing on the breath makes me uncomfortable. It is perhaps due to my being born premature. I struggled to breathe in the early days of my life and was on oxygen support. Whenever focusing on breath makes me uncomfortable, I focus on the sensations of the body. I try to accept them. Now this is happening. Now that is happening. I try not to react to them or try to alter them. After a while, I notice that the breath becomes slow and steady. Whenever you do that you are actually starting with the physical end of the physical–vital boundary. I have an ideating mind. It is harder for me to observe thoughts without following them. Focusing on an esoteric image or sound seems too repetitive for me. I have not seriously tried the Vichara Marga. Sometimes it occurs to me as to who is it that is breathing and who is it that is observing. If the breathing stops, how long the observer can observe?

Personally, after the practice of meditation, my bodily awareness has increased. I have realized that my body is hollowed with more open spaces than I originally thought. I have also felt my hand and feet have become larger. It has felt similar to how the tongue feels food particles. One gets a sensation of dealing with a large object. I practice this meditation lying on my back. I have felt the head and spine vividly with the body and limbs as an envelope around it. Sometimes the body feels light and ready to leap. Subjectively, I have felt much calmer.

I would urge the reader to practice meditation if it works for them. At no point in the practice of meditation, gloss over, deny or suppress thoughts or feelings. Creating a normative superego that judges the self for not getting it right is the opposite of well-being. If these thoughts, feelings and reactions fall away on their own like ripe fruits, you've got it right. If they do not, don't feel miserable. Utilize the other tools in this book.

10

The Route and Milestones to Well-being

How We Came Here?

Our route map to well-being is just about complete. We have broadly defined our goal as happiness and well-being in the sense of eudemonia and less as a high or a hedonic state. We don't want to split hairs between peace, tranquillity, a zest for life, meaning, connectedness, clarity, feet on ground and going about life in happy anticipation. We want all of it. Why not? We can have all of it. If you already have them in your life, you can seek more. The happy person can become happier. A normal life can become extraordinary. The science and art of this journey is what this book is all about.

We started the journey by surveying the external circumstances that a corporate professional or entrepreneur deals with in today's age. It is utterly simplistic to assume that these external factors can be solved. By understanding their impact on well-being, we can certainly mitigate it. We can make more specific decisions about them. My experience observing numerous instances could help you out in a dilemma with reference to these external stressors.

The inner theatres of individuals are not blank slates. There are numerous predispositions that can make us stew in worry, fret in anxiety and wallow in guilt and self-pity. These numerous dispositions again may make us feel like we don't belong, or feel ridiculed or threatened. Several of them may be legitimate fears and anxieties. Our difficult past may have given rise to feelings of guilt and self-pity. Several of our present-moment stressors like feeling bullied or ignored or ridiculed may be justifiable threat perceptions. Or maybe it is our inner chatter introducing an excessive reaction. We find out by doing an honest self-assessment. We understand that we have built these psychological defences to cope with big stressors. These psychological defences now justify every reaction by externalizing that the world is problematic. If our reactions are frequently one-dimensional, maybe it is time to scan the distortions in ourselves?

It turns out that we are not the only imperfect persons. Almost all of humanity suffers from distortions. Why? They served to increase our chances of survival. They helped us react quickly to the dangers of the forest. In our comfortable homes and offices, these very same instincts now distort our views and choices. Alright, so what do we do? We can minimize our errors and make our choices more logical by following the tips and tricks to overcome these universal distortions.

A wrong word or an accidental gesture can reveal our individual-specific conflict at work. These off-track actions when followed can provide insights into what we know and want but won't acknowledge. Every time you swallow, such undigested experiences scar you, make you defensive and feel less well about yourself and the world. Evidence that you are less alive and present can also be found in the way you transact with others. There are some patterns in the way we swallow and the way we interact. These lead to suboptimal selves and a suboptimal life. The tools of error and TA help you get on track.

As we scan deeper and farther, we discover how we teem with scars and contradictions. With effort and courage, we can peer into these depths. The searchlights of dreams help us access the unfathomable wonder that is our unconscious. It is a matter of awe how the ripples and bubbles on the surface actually originate deep inside. The cocktail of feelings and images are the night-time dreams we have when our oceanic selves absorb the streams of experience of the day. If we can access this awesome power, we can see the world and ourselves much more clearly. This flushes the neurosis off our minds. We can reach the pinnacle of well-being.

The swallowing we do with the experiences of the day not only settles down into the oceanic unconscious, they deposit undesirable elements in our bodies too. It is almost like they pass through the rarefied waters of the mind and get stuck in the mud of the body. Each of them, the mind and body can be utilized to shake ourselves clear of these undesirable elements.

We explore the twilight zone when mind meets matter through the biochemistry of happiness. These problems have been tackled and tackled well by the blue zoners of the world. To them, we turn and discover useful protocols of living.

We explore the different forms of meditation as a method of clearing the smokescreen. Meditation can create in us a buffer zone from which to view and lead a well-lived life. Meditation actually strengthens the twilight zone between mind and body. There is an extraordinary amount of evidence for us to take this seriously.

The self-assessment in this book should tell you about your risks and opportunities to happiness. The tools, tips and explanations should help you pursue a happier life.

Can We Measure Our Progress?

As you internalize the perspectives in the book and implement the tools and tips, you should observe visible progress. The signs of progress will be visible in multiple areas of life. Some signs will appear earlier than others. This is dependent on your own starting point.

1. **Self-acceptance**
   You will notice that you are observing reactions, some of them 'unthinkable' and which were suppressed earlier. You would have a greater sense of humour about yourself. You will take yourself less seriously in the larger scheme of things. You will have realizations in the course of the day, 'aha, this is why I am like this'.

2. **Proportional reactions**
   As self-acceptance increases, your reactions will be proportional than extreme. You will react; nay respond to situations more and more like the way you would have responded to something that happened 5 years ago.

There will be maturity and proportion in your response. You will be able to see the impact as if it is on someone else and logically reason out. You will be less swayed and driven by your own boiling self.

3. **Ability to switch off**

You would be fully absorbed in something and then switch off. When you pick it up again, you would not have thought about it in the intervening period, at least not consciously. You will begin to think more and worry less. Your weekends and vacations will complete move away from work and other preoccupations. You will be fully present to yourself and others in the weekends and in vacations.

4. **Decisive calls on the controllable factors**

If the matter is under your control and you can do something about it, you will think and act decisively. It does not matter if the decision is wrong; you will learn the lesson and move on. If the matter is not controllable, you will not sit and wish what others should do and how circumstances should help. When an uncontrollable situation becomes fortuitously controllable, you will swing into decisive response. In this way, you will develop a stoic approach.

5. **Accurate decision-making**

There is no guarantee that we will get all our decisions right. We will certainly get more decisions right than before. We will not be distracted by immediate circumstance while taking a long-term decision or a decision where the immediate circumstance has little bearing. We will understand and distinguish between the intensity of an outcome versus the probability of an outcome. You will provide for losses and not be unduly constrained by the fear of loss.

6. **Bounce back from setbacks**

   Should there be a setback, you will have already thought of how to live through it. It will come less as a surprise and more as an anticipated event. You would have found your safety nets and the tortoise shell into which you can temporarily retreat. You will even look at this phase of life as a chance to be heroic. You will work your way back with dignity and without undue self-sympathy.

7. **Easy and confident body language**

   Your body language would be warm, confident and expansive. It will connote that of a peace-loving giant. The elephant is a good metaphor. It knows its strength and does not go about proving it. You will listen with interest and be a source of security to those around you. Your body language will be surer and not tentative.

8. **Ability to sleep deeply**

   There will be pronounced stage 3 and stage 4 in your sleep cycle and it will occur in each of the 4–6 sleep cycles you would go through every night. When you wake up, you will feel much rested and rejuvenated. If you wear a device that measures quantity and quality of sleep, there will be marked improvement in the readings.

9. **Lucid dreams**

   You would reach a stage when you will begin to have lucid dreams. These are dream moments when you know that you are dreaming even while dreaming. You will perceive an ability to even direct the course of your dreams. You will not exercise this power as you want to know how your mind is working. You would become non-neurotic even in the dream state.

10. Feeling connected

You will be able to see another person as an individual like yourself with all the complexities and desires. You will be able to perceive the common destiny of all of us. You would be able to do business without being psychologically demanding. You will more easily accept another person, warts and all. You will be able to elicit the cooperation that our prehistoric ancestors elicited, in intensity and spirit. Depending on your own personality, you will either wish them well or let them be.

11. Feeling secure, grateful

Without counting on it, you will be able to relish the opportunities that chance and other people brought to you. There are very few individuals who can contemplate life this way. This alone is a good enough reason to feel grateful. You will also know that the same chance can bring misfortune but you will have the courage to heroically encounter it. The fact that you can direct your response to circumstance, however adverse, will give you a great sense of security. You know that even if things go wrong, you know how to suffer and yet be happy.

12. Focused and relaxed efforts

Your efforts towards your goals will be well directed. You would enjoy putting in focused efforts. At the same time, they will have the characteristic of play—an engaged play. They won't have the characteristic of a furrowed brow and perspiration. They will be to win as well as to play. The true test is if you are at your best that you can be today. Most days, your answer to the question will be yes. When you look back, you won't regret not having tried enough. Sure, there are lessons to learn. But, there won't be silly misses or lethargic procrastinations.

13. Mindfulness

You will be able to listen even at the busiest of moments. Listen to the way the morsel of food gets into your gut, listen to yourself and others breathe, listen to the multitudinous sensations in your body. You will be able to listen to your thoughts and feelings and the subtle likes and dislikes that they express all the time. Even if you lose your cool, you will see yourself losing it and not lose it for long. This will bring an element of cheer in the way you see yourself and the world.

14. Zest

There won't be a thing that is not offering an opportunity to relish. A zestful mind and body allows you to be in awe and engagement with what you encounter. Like Sherlock Holmes, since you see more and notice more, even ordinary events will be extraordinarily interesting. Since your interests will be manifold, you will have the opportunity to engage happily in many things.

15. Neither excited nor bored

While zest characterizes your interaction with the world, there will be a time and place for quiet predictability. Some of the most zestful people have ordered their lives so much that this predictability gives them the space to explore. Freud, for example, went through the same route from his home to his clinic and back. You will value boredom and predictability. Today, children like to be excited by external stimuli all the time, giving rise to attention-deficit hyperactivity disorders.

When a child or even an adult learns to experience excitement by the way they think about events and their connections, they are mentally healthy. They don't need a noisy, nervous, ever-changing landscape. They can elicit play out of the simplest of tools and items. They don't need the fanciful toys to stimulate them in multiple ways.

16. Seeing the world as it is

A clear appreciation of the world, oneself and one's circumstance is the pinnacle of mental health. Swami Vivekananda alludes to this when he describes Krishna of the Mahabharata. 'No cobwebs in the brain, no superstitions.' Krishna could utilize every humble person and every little circumstance in an effortless way to the agenda of establishing righteousness. By separating what one thinks of oneself and what must happen to what is really happening, an individual gets the highest chance of learning and development. You no longer stake your ego in everything you do. You can form accurate opinions about yourself by looking at a broader timeframe and outcome. Regardless of the outcome, you know you have to be gentle to yourself because you do have a place in the world.

17. Heroic and Humble

The ability to think free thoughts, the fact you possess a rational mind and your ability to possess your mind in the most adverse circumstance makes you heroic. The fact that our place in the cosmos is one little spot in one little moment makes you humble. Individual dignity comes from free thoughts and a possessed mind while humility comes from the finitude of our lives. That all of us will be forgotten is the real truth and that a few of us can contemplate this and lead courageous lives is the point of it all.

What Next?

As more and more people become more and more happy, they will create architecture for happiness in life. They will structure and order life in society so that everyone is happy. There will be more and more blue zones in the world. Individually, they will experience a kind of peak freedom and joy which is now a distant ideal.

Evolving the Well-being Protocol

As this science and art of happiness is critiqued, practised and improved, we can start an extraordinary revolution. It will follow a similar course like exercise. This too will be for everyone—the unhappy, the normal person and even to the happy to become happier. Corporations, resident associations, the government and of course the individuals will focus to develop the well-being protocol. Architects will design spaces for promoting pro-social behaviours. Doctors will treat the whole person and try to make them happy. Teachers will segregate students and give them each a different way to get happier based on their starting points. Leaders can measure if their countries became happier in their tenures.

Like the right to food, the right to livelihood, the right to breathe clean air, there will be a right to happiness. That day is much nearer than we think. At the centre of these efforts will be clarity of self, removal of all delusions, acceptance and gentle direction of the human condition to a greater good.

Bibliography

American Psychiatric Association. *Diagnostic and Statistical Manual of Mental Disorders.* Washington, DC: American Psychiatric Association, 2014. Available at: https://dsm. psychiatryonline.org (accessed 20 May 2018).

Ariely, D. *Predictably Irrational: The Hidden Forces that Shape Our Decisions.* New York, NY: Harper Collins, 2008.

Barett, Lisa Feldmann. 'You Aren't at the Mercy of Your Emotions—Your Brain Creates Them.' New York, NY: TED, 2018. Available at: https://www.ted.com/talks/lisa_feldman_barrett_you_aren_t_at_the_mercy_of_your_emotions_your_brain_creates_them (accessed 20 May 2018).

Bergland, Christopher. 'The Athlete's Way.' Available at: https://www.psychologytoday.com/us/blog/the-athletes-way/201803/how-does-vagusstoff-vagus-nerve-substance-calm-us-down (accessed 20 May 2018).

Berne, E. *Games People Play.* New York, NY: Ballantine Books/ Random house, (1965)1996.

———. *What Do You Say After You Say Hello.* London: Corgi Books, 1975.

Brugmann, J. *Welcome to the Urban Revolution.* New York, NY: Harper Collins, 2009.

Buddhaghoṣa. *Visuddhimagga: The Path of Purification.* Translated from Pali by Bhikkhu Nanamoli. Kandy: Buddhist Publication Society, 2011.

Buettner, Dan. *The Blue Zones: 9 Lessons for Living Longer from People Who've Lived the Longest.* Washington, DC: National Geographic Society, (2008)2012.

Campbell, J. *The Hero with a Thousand Faces.* Novato, CA: New World Library, (1949)2008.

Csikzentmihalyi, M. *Flow: The Psychology of Optimal Experience.* New York, NY: Harper Perennial Modern Classics, 2008.

Cuddy, Amy. *Your Body Language May Shape Who You Are.* New York, NY: TED, 2011. TED Talks: www.ted.com.

Dixon, K. H., and H. Kollias. 'The Ketogenic Diet: Does It Live Up To the Hype?' Available at: https://www.precisionnutrition.com/ketogenic-diet (accessed 20 May 2018).

Dobelli, R. *The Art of Thinking Clearly*. Translated by Nicky Griffin. London: Sceptre Books, 2013.

———. *The Art of the Good Life*. Translated by Caroline Waight. London: Sceptre Books, 2017.

Epictetus. *The Enchiridion (Manual of Living)*. Edited by Tom Crawford. London: Dover Publications, 2004.

Faraday, Ann. *The Dream Game*. New York, NY: Perennial Library/Harper and Row, 1976.

Festinger, L., and J. M. Carlsmith. 'Cognitive Consequences of Forced Compliance.' *Journal of Abnormal and Social Psychology* 58, no. 2 (1959): 203–11.

Frankl, Victor E. *Man's Search for Meaning: The Classic Tribute to Hope from the Holocaust*. London: Ebury Publishing, (1946)2004.

Freud, S. *A General Introduction to Psychoanalysis*. pdfbooksworld through creative commons license, 1920.

———. *The Interpretation of Dreams*. 3rd and revised English ed. New York, NY: Harper Collins, 1931.

———. *The Origin of Religion*, Volume 13. Edited by Albert Dickson, Pelican Freud Library. UK: Penguin, 1985.

———. *The Psychopathology of Everyday Life*. Translated by A. A. Brill. London: Dover Publications (1914)2003.

———. *Civilization and Its Discontents*. Translated by David McLintock. London: Penguin books, 2003.

Gilbert, Dan. 'The Psychology of Your Future Self.' New York, NY: TED, 2004. TED Talks: www.ted.com/dan_gilbert_you_are_always_changing.

Greater Good Science Center. *Raisin Meditation: Eating one Raisin*. Berkeley, CA: University of Berkeley. Available at: https://ggia.berkeley.edu/practice/raisin_meditation# (accessed 20 May 2018).

Hammond, Martin, trans. *Marcus Aurelius, Meditations*. London: Penguin Classics, 2006.

Harris, T. A. *I'm OK, You Are OK*. London: Arrow Books/Random House, (1967)1995.

Holiday, R., and S. Hanselman. *The Daily Stoic: 366 Meditations on Wisdom, Perseverance and the Art of Living*. London: Profile Books, 2016.

Iyengar, B. K. S. *The Light of Yoga*, 33rd impression. Noida: Harper Collins India, (1966)2015.

Kahneman, D. *Thinking Fast and Slow*, International Edition. London: Penguin press, (2011)2015.

Keng, S. L., M. J. Smoski, and C. J. Robins. 'Effects of Mindfulness on Psychological Health: A Review of Empirical Studies.' *Clinical Psychological Review* 31, no. 6 (2011): 1041–56.

Lehrer, P. M. and R. Gevirtz. 'Heart Rate Variability and Biofeedback: Why and How Does It Work?' *Frontiers in Psychology* 5 (2014): 756.

Lin, P., and H. M. Seiden. 'Mindfulness and Psychoanalytic Psychotherapy: A Clinical Convergence.' *Psychoanalytic Psychology* 32, no. 2 (April, 2015): 321–33.

Morris, D. *The Human Zoo*. New York, NY: Vintage, (1969)1994.

———. *The Naked Eye*. London: Ebury Press/Random House, 2000.

———. *People Watching*. New York, NY: Vintage (1977)2002.

Morris Rosendahl, Deborah J. 'Are There Anxious Genes?' *Dialogues in Clinical Neuroscience* 4, no. 3 (2002, September): 251–60.

Rajeswaran, Jamuna, and Catholyn N. Bennet. 'The *Neurophysiology of Stress*.' In Pestonjee, D. M., and S. Pandey (eds), *Stress and Work: Perspectives on Understanding and Managing* Stress. New Delhi: SAGE, 2013.

Rubin, G. *The Happiness Project*. New York: Harper, 2016.

Russell, B. *Mysticism and Logic: Including a Free Man's Worship*. Crows Nest: George Allen and Unwin Ltd, 1918.

———. *The Conquest of Happiness*. Routledge Classics, (1930)2006.

Seligman, Martin E. P. *Learned Optimism*. New York, NY: Vintage, 2006.

———. *Authentic Happiness*. New York, NY: Atria, (2002)2013.

———. *Flourish*. New York: Ataria, (2011)2013.

Sood, A. *The Mayo Clinic Guide to Stress-free Living*. Da Capo Press, 2013.

Szalavitz, Maia. 'The Biology of Kindness: How It Makes Us Healthier and Happier?' 2013. Available at: http://healthland.time.com/2013/05/09/why-kindness-can-make-us-happier-healthier/ (accessed 20 May 2018).

Thaler, R. H., and C. R. Sunstein. *Nudge: Improving Decisions about Health, Wealth and Happiness*. New York, NY: Penguin Books, 2009.

Twenge, J. M., T. E. Joiner, M. L. Rogers, and G. N. Martin. 'Increases in Depression Symptoms, Suicide-related Outcomes and Suicide Rates Among U.S. Adolescents After 2010.' *Clinical Psychological Science* 6, no. 1 (2018): 3–17.

United Nations Sustainable Development Solutions Network. *World Happiness Report 2018*. UN Report on Happiness. New York, NY: United Nations Sustainable Development Solutions Network, 2018. Available at: www.worldhappiness. report/ed/2018 (accessed 20 May 2018).

Walker, Matthew. *Why We Sleep: Unlocking the Power of Sleep and Dreams*. New York: Scribner, 2017.

Winget, C., and M. Kramer. *Dimensions of Dreams*. Florida: University Presses of Florida, 1979.

Zeldin, T. *An Intimate History of Humanity*. New York: Vintage Books/Random house, (1994)1998.

Zinn, Jon Kabat. *Full Catastrophe Living: Using the Wisdom of Your Body and Mind to Face Stress, Pin and Illnesses*. New York, NY: Bantam Books, (1979)2013.

About the Author

R. Anand is a practising HR leader with about two decades of experience. His keen study of human psychology and decision-making as well as his experience in counselling and developing hundreds of executives and thousands of professionals have been focused to answer this single question—can regular professionals like us attain happiness? He believes that not a dogmatic approach but a scientific approach to this question would help us achieve this.

He has received international and national acclaim for introducing social HR, alignment of individual drivers and the employee life cycle with engagement and performance as well as for skill and leadership development.

He has spoken at various TV shows and has published and has been featured in national journals, newspapers and magazines as well as international journals. An alumnus of IIT Madras and XLRI Jamshedpur, Anand serves on the National Board of NHRDN.

Heading global people practices, integration of an acquired business and hire-to-retire management of 27,000 professionals across 22 countries are responsibilities he discharged as Senior Vice President, Human Resources, at HCL Technologies. He is transitioning to be an independent consultant on HR, organizational effectiveness and in the development of a technology-assisted individual well-being protocol.

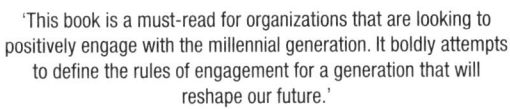